S0-AZB-360

7 TRAITS

How to change your world

SHALOM DENBO

Copyright 2015 by Shalom Denbo

All rights reserved. No part of this book may be reproduced in any
form or by any electronic or mechanical means, including
information storage and retrieval systems, without permission in
writing from the publisher, except by a reviewer who may quote
brief passages in a review.

First Edition: May 2015

Cover design by Saul Blinkoff and Dalia Haimen
Author Photo by Jonah Light

Printed in the United States of America

In memory of Rabbi Noach Weinberg

Who believed I could change the world

Contents

7 TRAITS

Introduction
Learning To Fly

"Give me ten men and I'll change the world."
Rabbi Noah Weinberg

The first time I heard those words I knew I wanted to be a part of that dream.

"Change the world!"

Who wouldn't want to be involved in something that big? We all want to be great. Have you ever heard anyone say, "No thanks, I'll settle for being average"? Of course not. Why strive for mediocrity?

That same yearning for greatness is why we love movies with heroes. We connect with all types of heroes – not just the super heroes from the comics. We especially relate to movies where the hero is an average person who triumphs over challenges thrown in his way. We are drawn to these stories because our hearts are engraved with the deep understanding that we are all created for greatness and that we have the ability to realize that potential. Those stories inspire us with hopes, aspirations and the desire to break out of our boxes so we can accomplish something much more than merely existing. Ultimately, this is one of the basic desires of every human being. Each one of us wants to know that we matter, that our life makes a difference. That is the secret behind the magic of the movies. Watching an ordinary person go out and save the world shows us who we can become.

When I was a boy I had a secret desire to be able to fly. I don't mean in an airplane – anyone can do that. I mean actually fly. Looking back, it seems amusing, but at the time I was absolutely serious. I used to stay up late at night and pray to be able to fly. I used to promise that I wouldn't tell anyone and that I would only use that power to help people (right after I took care of the bully down the street and impressed the girl I had a crush on). What I know now is that my desire to be able to fly was actually a desire to be unique. I wanted something that would express my singular identity. I imagine most of us had similar dreams and fantasies as children. The tragedy is that we let go of those dreams instead of understanding their message – the message that each one of us has a unique contribution to bring to the world. If only we could learn how to connect to that part of our soul, life would be exhilarating. It would be as if we really were flying. Living like that would definitely change our world.

When I was 22, I left the United States for Jerusalem in search of meaning and spirituality. I was hoping to find someone that could teach me how to fly. I ended up in the Old City of Jerusalem with Rabbi Noah Weinberg, of blessed memory. For the next seven years of my life I had the privilege of staying there and learning from his wisdom. His words changed my life. With every fiber of his being, Rabbi Weinberg believed it was possible to change the world, and he lived with the understanding that each one of us has the potential to achieve greatness. He never stopped telling his students – and in fact, anyone who would listen – that everyone has the power to change the world.

One of the key lessons Rabbi Weinberg taught was that each one of us should remind ourselves every day that the world was created for me. Imagine what life would look like if we realized that the entire world, in all of its glory, was created in order to help us achieve our unique purpose. Sadly, most of us get so caught up in petty nonsense or the daily monotony of life that we end up just trying to make it through another day. We lose sight of our driving desire to know that our lives are relevant and that we can make a difference.

Rabbi Weinberg used to declare that if he had those ten men he would change the world. I never understood why he said this. Here was a man who, with nothing but the power of his dream, built an international organization dedicated to Jewish education. Few people in history have changed the face of the Jewish world as Rabbi Weinberg did. He created an army of dedicated teachers whose sole mission was to help spread the wisdom of Judaism to the world. How could he possibly think that he lacked ten men? Surely, he had hundreds – if not thousands – of soldiers in his army!

One day I summoned the courage to ask him what he meant. His answer changed my life.

The reason Rabbi Weinberg did not feel he had ten men was that his understanding of manhood meant taking responsibility for the whole world – not just our personal projects or efforts. Being responsible for the world meant that there was no room for mediocrity, only greatness. After hearing this, I realized I fell short. A man, he explained, masters the seven traits that are the subject of this book.

What does it mean to change the world? Should we all run off and try to stop world hunger? Does changing the world obligate us to sacrifice ourselves for causes that intrinsically are global in nature? Or does changing the world simply mean taking responsibility for our own lives and the lives of those around us? How we choose to change the world and answer those questions is left for each one us to decide. However, one thing is certain: Being a man requires us to be concerned with the world outside of our own boundaries and helping to improve it to the best of our abilities.

Regardless of which path we choose, whether it is to change the whole world or to take responsibility for our own personal world, the seven traits outlined in this book represent what it takes to achieve that goal. Taking responsibility means that we must do everything in our power to see to it that it gets done. Every human being knows that we live below our potential. We all know that we could accomplish much more. We all know we could be great. These seven traits are the tools to help us get there.

While this is not a religious book, it is based on Jewish wisdom. I have tried to make those ideas tangible and relevant to any reader, without regard to religious identity or observance. To whatever extent these ideas are confusing and inaccurate, that is merely a reflection of my inability to express them properly. Please do not mistake my deficiencies for a deficiency in the depth and meaning of these powerful and time-honored lessons.

Steve Jobs once said the people who are crazy enough to think they can change the world are the ones who do it. Each one of us can change our world. Each one of us can tap into our own uniqueness and fly. Rabbi Weinberg lived with that understanding every day. This book is the answer he gave me on how we can live that way too.

ONE

Five Finger Clarity

"Our doubts are traitors and make us lose the good we oft might win, by fearing to attempt."
William Shakespeare

Five Finger Clarity

How many fingers do you have on your hand? Five. Knowing an answer to any question as clear as that is called five-finger clarity. That is the kind of clarity we must have when tackling a task as great as changing the world. It requires a clear vision of what it is that we want to accomplish and why. It also requires a road map for how to get there. In other words, we must have clarity.

On the surface, what I'm saying may seem obvious. However, gaining clarity is often easier said than done. In order to demonstrate what I mean, let's try a second question. Off the top of your head, what are the three most important lessons you have learned about life? By the time we reach adulthood, most of us should be able to answer this question without too much difficulty. Or perhaps the answer did not come so easily. One thing is most probably true: it took a lot more time to answer this question than knowing how many fingers you have. Yet, if we truly had acquired a number of lessons that could serve as a guide for our life, we ought to be able to articulate them as quickly as how many fingers are on our hand. Lack of clarity is the reason we are unable to do so.

The Founding Fathers of America had clarity. In 1775, one of those Founding Fathers, Patrick Henry, declared, "Give me liberty or give me death!" That is a tremendous statement of clarity and conviction. Rabbi Weinberg used to borrow from that quote and declare, "Give me clarity or give me death." Without clarity we cannot possibly hope to achieve the most life has to offer. Imagine the frustration of trying to put together a 500-piece puzzle without a picture on the cover. Without that image the pieces of the puzzle are a jumble of chaos. Similarly, without an overall vision for our lives, the puzzle pieces of life can seem like senseless details that have no real relation to each other. Imagine how frustrating it would be to be hired by a company without ever being given a proper job description. We could easily end up spending our time performing tasks that seem to be important, only to find out that we have been wasting our efforts on worthless or unimportant tasks while important matters remain undone. This is what life is like when we lack clarity, constant frustration and disappointment.

We live in a time when one distraction after another prevents us from gaining clarity. Our senses are bombarded from every side, without rest. We rarely have a moment to stop and think. From the moment we open our eyes until our heads hit the pillow at night, we move from one thing to the next. Day after day we repeat the same routine. Rare is the moment when we allow ourselves the simple luxury of thought and contemplation. Everywhere we turn, we are able to entertain ourselves into oblivion – the radio in the car, the T.V. or internet at home, the smart phone in the elevator and everywhere else. This trend does not appear to be slowing down anytime soon.

We no longer allow ourselves even to think about trivial matters. In an age of instant information, everything has to have an immediate response. If we don't know the answer to a question, we simply look it up on our phones. How can we be expected to achieve clarity surrounded by such mental laziness and chaos? Studies have shown that even though this tech-savvy generation has a greater ability to multi-task, the quality of each individual task we perform is rapidly diminishing. The consequence of all this additional stimuli is that we focus less and less on setting aside undisturbed time just to think.

Not only is there a lack of clarity and often confusion but we are consumed by a constant nagging sense of doubt. We suffer from both internal and external doubt. Internally, we struggle with an existential angst and anxiety that results from our innate desire for greatness. We know that we possess the intellectual and emotional capacities to grow and accomplish great things in this world. On the one hand, this immense potential is the source of our happiness and fulfillment. On the other hand, the awareness that our talents and gifts are not being used to their fullest capacity generates an emptiness we can feel in the marrow of our bones. This awareness can overwhelm us with the thought that perhaps we will never reach our full potential. This fear, together with an unpredictable future, creates a constant sense of emotional turmoil.

Although we might not always be consciously aware of this internal fear, it resides within us and eats away at our self-confidence. We fill ourselves with negative thoughts and dismiss any notion of accomplishing anything with statements such as "it can't be done," "it won't work" or "someone already tried that and failed."

Externally, fear and doubt afflict us when we are confronted with the pessimism that is so prevalent in society today. There is no shortage of cynics who try to convince us that we cannot accomplish anything meaningful. These cynics tell us that our goals and expectations are unrealistic, and unfortunately we have a tendency to believe them. They dismiss our dreams as outlandish or simply the folly of youth, and we allow ourselves to believe they are right. As a result of these combined sources of doubt we are left in a state of confusion. Decisions that need to be made weigh heavily on us. How are we to know what is the right thing to choose? This uncertainty and insecurity has spawned an attitude of pessimism that is so pervasive that the world has come to call it simply being "realistic."

We Need Purpose

With so much doubt, no wonder we lack clarity in the most crucial areas of life. So let's start with the basics: One of the most basic needs of every human being is to know that life has purpose and meaning. We see this from the Torah's written account of the story of creation. The placement of Adam in the Garden of Eden is repeated twice. In the original Hebrew, two different words are used to describe each time Adam was placed in the garden. In the first version, the Hebrew word used to describe Adam's placement in the garden implies a casual and temporary placement, whereas the subsequent narrative uses a word that indicates a greater sense of permanence. There is only one other difference between the two accounts. In the second account, we are told the reason why Adam has been placed in the garden, namely, to work it and guard it. The second version, gives Adam his purpose and thus his permanence. Without that sense of purpose, man was not at rest in the garden, and it was as if he did not belong there.

Without meaning and purpose in our life, we feel lost, as if we are wandering aimlessly through existence. Tragically, one of the most common questions asked by people contemplating suicide is why they should bother going on living. The need for meaning and purpose in life is so great that without it the pain of life is almost too great to bear. Friedrich Nietzsche said, "He who has a why to live can bear almost any how." It is so crucial to have meaning that we often create arbitrary sources of that meaning. That is why Rabbi Moshe Chaim Luzzatto wrote in his classical philosophical treatise *The Path of the Just* that "the foundation of life is for a person to have clarity as to what he is living for."

Definitions Lead to Wisdom

Clarity comes from the acquisition of wisdom. Wisdom is more than mere knowledge. There are many forms of knowledge. A person can have vast knowledge of the animal kingdom, with the ability to enumerate all the various species and their dietary habits, and yet still lack wisdom. Similarly, there is a grand disparity between wisdom and intelligence. History is replete with individuals who were praised for their brilliance but lived despicable lives or advocated for morally repugnant philosophies. Wisdom is the knowledge and understanding of life and all its relationships. It is the understanding of the big picture. It comes from a combination of a good dose of actual education and a wealth of experience. As Robin Williams' character says in the 1997 film *Good Will Hunting*, and I am paraphrasing; "you can quote a sonnet but you know nothing about love, because you haven't lived it." At the same time, while experience is essential to wisdom, intellectual understanding cannot be minimized nor substituted, and is still crucial for obtaining clarity.

In order to become wise we must learn to be intellectuals. To some people, the term "intellectual" carries a negative connotation. In the context of this discussion, an intellectual is someone who leads with his head instead of his heart. An intellectual lives through his understanding of himself and the world around him. An intellectual is proactive as opposed to reactive. On the other hand, when our emotions dictate our decisions we live in a constant state of reacting to the world around us, rather than proactively engaging the world with our mind.

The first step toward becoming an intellectual is to define our terms. A lack of definitions for the key ideas and terms we use leaves us vulnerable to emotional responses and only complicates matters. The power of definitions lies in their ability to isolate and identify core issues and concepts. How many times has a disagreement escalated into a full-blown argument simply because the people involved failed to clarify exactly what they were arguing about? How many marriages or business partnerships have dissolved simply because the partners neglected to define what they meant by happiness or success? When it comes to comments and discussions regarding our values we often throw around words that can be insulting and hurtful. For example, a parent might accuse a child of being pigheaded or stubborn – while the child simply sees himself as "demonstrating his independence." Who is right? An objective observer would mention that it depends on your definition of "pigheaded" or 'independent." A wife may complain that her husband is stingy – while her husband truly believes he is simply being "frugal" or "economically efficient." Again, restoring peace to the couple depends, at least in part, on defining what each person means by his or her terms. Anytime we have a disagreement, the first thing we should do is refrain from throwing accusatory labels at each other and agree to define our terms.

Furthermore, we cannot begin to understand ourselves and acquire clarity until we define the terms we use to describe ourselves. In order to express ourselves properly, we need to gain an objective insight into the thoughts and emotions we think and feel. Emotionally, we like the idea of being an intellectual, so we brand ourselves as such. We are enamored by the concept of love, so we make statements such as "I love you" casually. If we had to choose between being happy or rich, the majority of us would most likely choose happy – yet we spend the majority of our time and energy trying to get ahead financially. Definitions allow us to honestly understand the essence of these desires and measure our commitment with integrity.

Here are two examples:

Love: an emotion we feel when we recognize and identify a person with his or her virtues.

Love is not a happening. It is a choice we have the ability to make. It is often said that love is blind. Nothing could be further from the truth! If anything, love is a magnifying glass. *Infatuation* is blind. Ask any high school quarterback why he loves a cheerleader, and you'll get a pretty good idea what I mean. If I were to ask your mother to tell me three character traits or habits you need to improve upon, and she was anything like my mother, she would most likely answer, "Only three?!" At the same time, if I were to ask her to tell me about you, she would probably refrain from mentioning any of those much-needed "areas of improvement." Why? Is she blind to them? Of course not. She loves you – and therefore, she does not identify you with your flaws.

On the other hand, we all have someone we don't like, a person that bothers us immensely. If you think about that person right now I'm sure you immediately identified two or three specific habits that annoy you the most about that person. Put that person aside for a moment, and now think about someone you love. Realize that this second person also has two or three annoying habits, although I'm sure you are smiling right now as you think of your friend's. What's the difference? The difference is that we tend forgive the bad habits of people we love and identify them with their positive traits, as opposed to people we don't like, whom we tend to associate with their negative characteristics.

Happiness: an emotion we feel when we focus on and appreciate what we have acquired or experienced.

The secret to achieving happiness is realizing that it is a choice and not a happening. Most people are waiting for something to happen in order to make them happy. It could be a new car, a new job, a new relationship, etc. No matter what that thing is, the focus is on what we don't have. The sad reality is that if we are not happy with what we already have, it is unlikely that we will be happy with whatever we get. We can choose to be happy by realizing how many blessings we do have and learning how to appreciate them, rather than worrying about what we wish we had instead.

Clearly, we have only touched the surface when it comes to pursuing love or happiness. However, I think you will agree that even these basic definitions carry the power to profoundly change our attitude toward life. Yet, in my years of teaching, I have found that even though most people will actually agree that they are true – they will still fail to apply them in their lives. Instead of recognizing that real change takes consistent effort and concentration, most people quickly revert back to their determination that you can't define love or happiness!

The Battle for Life is the Battle for Sanity

That inevitable road to despair is precisely why the battle for life is the battle for sanity! Albert Einstein is widely credited with noting that the definition of insanity is "doing the same thing over and over again while expecting different results." We all know that overeating makes us feel sick, and yet we still go ahead and eat too much. We all know that if we wake up early, jump out of bed and attack the day, we feel more alive and accomplished than if we sleep in late and lie around the house doing nothing. There's no greater sign of insanity than knowing something to be true and still actively contradicting it. Yet we do this all the time. We make the same mistakes over and over again and then wonder why. Why do we continue to do things that make us miserable? The reason is obvious. People are crazy! It is part of the human condition to carry around a certain amount of insanity. Sometimes we excuse ourselves by promising things will be different next time. Other times, we choose to ignore many of those "truths we hold to be self-evident" in favor of chilling out. The problem is when we allow all of these little acts of insanity to add up until they overtake our life. You can only ignore your own principles for so long before it starts to hurt. No one wants to make a career out of being insane.

If it is foolish to allow ourselves to distort our basic daily responsibilities, how much more so when it comes to our major life decisions? To put it bluntly: How can you change the world when you can't get out of bed in the morning? Combine that with the fact that life has so many obstacles, deterrents and struggles to begin with, and it becomes clear that clarity – true, solid, five-finger clarity – is the only weapon we have to defeat the insanity that surrounds us every day.

Some mistakes we would never make. If someone offered you a cyanide cocktail, my bet is you would refuse. Why is that? Clarity. When we know something so clearly, we don't ignore it. We act on it – and live. That is the power of Five Finger Clarity.

Having Clarity Means Knowing Oneself

If there is one area where having clarity is crucial, it is in knowing who we are. As my rabbi used to always say "If you don't know yourself, you don't know anything". Growth in life means learning how we function as human beings. Certain general principles apply to all human beings, regardless of gender, race or nationality. At the same time, each one of us possesses traits that are unique to us an individual. The more we understand and utilize these principles the greater success we will have in fulfilling our potential. The road to self-discovery is a profound and exhilarating journey, one that should last a lifetime. Only allowing ourselves to become numb to our basic human desire for greatness can stop us from pursuing this quest.

Often times the pressures of daily life can seem so overwhelming that finding the answer to the question of who we are can seem trivial or of secondary importance. However, only by understanding ourselves can we come to understand why we do what we do. Why do we lose motivation in our careers? Why do we allow our wife and children to take a back seat to our daily distractions? The more we know ourselves the more we can make sense of our reality. This awareness provides more than insight into our actions. It endows us with the necessary tool to persist, persevere, and ultimately succeed in accomplishing our life's goals. Therefore, knowing yourself is having clarity.

What am I Living For?

The most powerful question we can ask ourselves is, "What am I living for?" This is arguably the most crucial question a person can ask. Yet, the inability to respond with a coherent answer tempts us to change the subject. Having a lack of clarity on something as profound as the meaning of life can be disconcerting, to say the least. Nevertheless, it is still possible to gain clarity on this question as well. Even though our priorities may change as we go through life, being able to answer to this question is the foundation of our life and should remain a constant.

Several years ago I participated in an intense strategic planning conference. Most strategic planning sessions focus primarily on a mission statement, which is vital to an organization's success. However, this particular conference focused on another powerful aspect – values.

Every organization, corporation or person has values that form an integral part of who they are and what they stand for. Knowing these values not only helps us understand ourselves but more importantly empowers us to live by them. Our life's purpose should be built around our core values.

A powerful exercise in building clarity is to list our values. Make a list of values you hold to be true. After making this list go through each one and analyze why you believe that value to be true. To borrow from our previous illustration, do you know it to be true the way you know you have five fingers? How did you come to this knowledge? Do you simply desire it to be true and therefore have faith that it is so? Or perhaps society has influenced you to adopt this conviction?

Once you have clarity on your core values, you can then begin to create your life's mission statement. Just as having a mission statement is crucial for a company's success, each person must have a mission statement that guides the path to his own success. Each one of us should have a mission statement in the form of a clear, concise, articulate statement that sums up our life's purpose.

What's Worth Dying For?

If we really wish to understand who we are and what our life's purpose is, we need to know what we are living for. To truly understand what we are living for, all we need to do is ask ourselves another simple, yet very profound question: What am I willing to die for? If there is one thing our parents taught us, even if by default, it is that there is something worth dying for. Every one of us knows full well that if we bring a child into the world that child will one day die. Hopefully, that will be after a long life, but death is an inevitable consequence of life and yet our parents still chose to bring us into the world. It must be because something about life is worth dying for.

Now that we have been given life we must actually choose to live it. There is an old adage: "Everybody dies but not everybody lives." In order to live we must be able to determine the difference between simply existing and truly living. To simply exist means going through the motions of life with the intention of maximizing our comfort and maintaining complacency. Usually this comes at the expense of meaning and greatness. On the other hand, truly living means actively deciding to choose meaning and greatness. This, too, comes with a price – the price is foregoing comfort and complacency.

Why not just exist? If only it were that easy! The purpose of human life is not merely to exist. Everyone understands that it is better to die fighting for a worthy cause than to live for nothing, frittering away the years. When the Forefather of the Jewish People and the father of monotheism, Abraham, realized that the pagan understanding of the world was worthless, he attempted to enlighten those around him. At the time, the leader of the "civilized world" was the evil King Nimrod. Fearing Abraham's radical views could lead to revolution, Nimrod sought to crush Abraham and his ideas before they could take root. Nimrod arrested Abraham and presented him with an ultimatum: Either bow down to the God of Fire or be thrown into a fiery pit. Abraham unsuccessfully attempted to convince Nimrod to abandon his views, and chose not to bow down. Bowing down would mean admitting defeat and be tantamount to accepting the notion of a world with many gods.   Abraham refused to bow down. Nimrod threw Abraham into the furnace and a miracle took place, saving him from the flames. Abraham had made a choice though, that it would be better to die standing up for his values than to live a lie.

Figure out what you are willing to die for. That in and of itself is a profound awareness. But don't stop there. Once you understand what you are willing to die for, figure out how to live for it. The very values that you deem worthy of dying for should be the focus and purpose of why you are living. That is your mission statement.

Once you have that clarity, you can make it real by asking yourself three questions at the end of each day:

What did I do today that got me closer to that mission?

What did I do today that moved me further away from that mission?

What am I going to do tomorrow that will ensure I continue doing those things that get me closer and prevent me from doing those things that move me away?

Once we understand what we are living for, the next aspect of clarity is to establish goals – firm, concrete goals in as many areas as possible. Any serious business executive sets goals for his business and systematically gauges whether the company is making progress or not.   In the business world, goals are not merely wishful thinking or flowery aspirations, but the result of a definable and measurable vision set down by the leaders of the company. Yet, when it comes to the business of life, few people take the time to set real goals for themselves – beyond losing weight and making more money. Is that not tragic? Why should we avoid spending time outlining goals for all the other areas of our lives? What do you want to accomplish in your marriage? As a parent? What character traits do you value and wish to develop? Take time to make an actual list of these goals, rather than relying on clichés and platitudes. One word of caution: While these goals should be as concrete and measurable as possible, avoid setting yourself up for failure by setting goals that are unrealistic or too daunting for your current situation. Instead, the best recipe for success should encompass goals that can be achieved in small, incremental and measured steps. That is the Jewish approach to achieving greatness, which can be understood with even more clarity by the following analogy. According to Judaism, when we die we will be shown the obstacles we were meant to overcome in our lifetime. These obstacles were the various challenges and tests intended to make us great. For those who were successful, the obstacles will be piled one on top of the other, on top of the other, until the accumulation of challenges appears as high as the highest mountain. As they strain their necks to view to the top of this massive mountain, these people will stand in awe that they were ever able to reach such heights. And for those who gave in? To these people, the obstacles will be spread out on the ground, looking no more formidable than stepping over a thread of hair. As they survey the landscape of their life, they will lament how it was possible that they failed to take such a small step. The answer to each of these two groups of people, the triumphant and the defeated, is in how we view the challenge in front of us. If we focus only on the monumental nature of the task at hand, we will end up feeling overwhelmed and all attempts will be defeated. If, on the other hand, we recognize that the only way to climb a mountain is to take it one step at a time, then we are much more likely able to reach the summit. The way to climb a mountain is to see the whole mountain as the ultimate goal, and then set our sights on small incremental steps. That is how we should set goals.

As we continue through the next six traits it is important to understand that each of them depends on clarity. Each subsequent trait will only be useful if we have clarity both on what our purpose is, and in the knowledge that these are the traits necessary to achieve that purpose. Before going on, make sure you have worked through this chapter so that the next time you are asked to list the most important lessons you have learned in life you will not hesitate for even a second before answering.

Clarity or Death

- Make a list of the three most important lessons you have learned about life.
- Make a list of values that are an integral part of your life and define them.
- Write out your life's mission statement by asking yourself, "What am I willing to die for?"
- Map out life goals for the next year, five years and ten years.
- Ask yourself every day the following three questions:

    1. What did I do today that got me closer to my life's mission?

    2. What did I do today that moved me further away from that mission?

    3. What am I going to do tomorrow that will ensure I continue doing those things that get me closer and prevent me from doing those things that move me away?

Responsibility

"The price of greatness is responsibility."
Winston Churchill

Clarity in life is crucial, but it is only the first step. The second trait in becoming a man is to understand that life has obligations. It is not merely that we choose to take responsibility, it is that we must do so.

Imagine the following scenario. You live and work in a quiet rural area. Everyday your walk to work goes through a path that has a footbridge over a river. One day while crossing the bridge someone below is screaming for help. However, you don't know how to swim, so all you can do is dial 911 on your cell phone, scream for help and look around for something to throw to the poor victim. Since you live so far from the police station, by the time the police come, the man drowns as you watch helplessly. Two days later the same thing occurs. Again you call 911, and again they arrive too late. A few days later the same scenario occurs a third time. Again you call 911, and, sadly, again they arrive too late. How much longer would you allow this to go on before you petition the city to put up a higher fence? How much longer could you live with yourself without taking swimming lessons? Why would you bother to do these things? *Because you can.* Once we are aware that we can, in fact, do something to improve a bad situation, we must act on it. As Voltaire said, "With great power comes great responsibility."

As our scenario of the drowning incidents shows, being able to do something does not mean we are responsible – it means we are obligated. We really must do something. It is incredibly praiseworthy to volunteer our time and energy to worthy causes. However, going beyond volunteering to the level of accepting obligation deserves even greater praise. By definition a volunteer remains a volunteer as long as he is interested or emotionally inclined to doing so. Taking on an obligation is a whole other ballgame. The requirement to meet our obligations has nothing to do with whether we feel like doing so or not. That is why they're called obligations. We can't just walk away.

As a husband and a father I have responsibilities that I must fulfill. A few years back I was flown into Sonoma Valley to help officiate a wedding. The wedding took place in an actual vineyard. The scenery was breathtaking. After the wedding I had a tremendous desire to rent a car and just drive for days through the wine country. Of course I could have, but not without abandoning my responsibilities to my wife and children, who were waiting for me to return to Los Angeles. When our responsibilities rise to the level of obligations, we know that unless there is a very good explanation, we cannot simply ignore them.

Anyone with a heart who hears about the suffering that exists in the world cannot help but be tempted to feel deep frustration, and sometimes even despair. We would never be so crass to just dismiss the realities of the world and say we don't care. We never ask "what difference is it to me that thousands of people died in the tsunami?" Instead, we rightfully empathize but dismiss our responsibility and ask "what can I possibly do?" However, there is a better way to respond, and it's very easy to do.   Instead of allowing ourselves to become jaded, all we have to do is ask ourselves one simple question: "What can I do to help?"

We all live with the profound reality that we are responsible for the world, but we just don't know what to do. We intuitively understand that if we could do something to make a difference then we are obligated to do so – but we deceive ourselves into thinking it is just too hard to figure out, too challenging to break out of our comfort zone, and too painful to make changes in the way we live. This is true whether we are talking about great global issues like war, starvation and disaster, or whether we are focused on our neighbor down the block. Having the ability to impact the world means that we have the responsibility to do so as well.

Get Rid of the Excuses

Even if we know it to be true that we need to take responsibility in our lives, that does not stop us from making all kinds of excuses for why we can't. We constantly push off to a later point what we should be taking care of right now. When I was young my father used to call me the 'alls I have ta' kid. Whenever my father would ask if I had taken care of my homework or my household responsibilities, my response would always be the same. Instead of owning up to the reality that I had not been responsible, I would give the same excuse each time. I would say that I'm basically done and 'alls I have ta do' is one more thing and then I'll be done. I was constantly pushing off my responsibilities, instead of just taking care of them right then and there.

Procrastination is just one type of excuse. Another common and destructive excuse is that we are incapable of accomplishing the task at hand.   An ancient Jewish story points this out beautifully. One time, Elijah the Prophet met up with a simple fisherman who had long since given up trying to master anything more than the very basics of life and was currently wasting time. Elijah asked him why was so determined to waste his potential and what explanation he would give to the Almighty when he passed from this world.

With great confidence, the fisherman responded that he had nothing to worry about, as he had a valid answer.

"What is it?" asked the prophet.

"God created me this way. He knows I don't have the ability to become a great scholar or understand the perplexities of life."

Recognizing that the man was a fisherman, Elijah began asking him questions about how to fish. The fisherman went on to explain in detail all the skills of fishing. What kind of bait to use. How to cast the line. The proper way to reel in the fish so it doesn't come off the hook. It turned out that simple fisherman who claimed to be unable to learn the wisdom of Torah was actually a genius when it came to the art of catching fish!

At the end of his detailed explanation, Elijah asked the fisherman, "You mean God gave you the intellect to know how to fish but not how to understand life?"

Immediately the fisherman realized that his whole life was nothing more than an excuse for not taking responsibility, and he began to weep. Elijah comforted him by telling him, "My son, do you think you are so different from everyone else? Every person leaves this world hoping to provide the same excuse – and every one of us will be shown that our own actions prove us wrong!"

Each one of us has all kinds of excuses for why we can't accomplish greatness and make a difference in our lives. Some of us blame our parents, others blame our teachers or our siblings or our friends. Many of us blame society, and when the going really gets rough – we ultimately blame God. However, when it comes to something we really want, whether trivial or meaningful, we always seem to find a way to make it happen. Remember when you wanted that new smartphone? No excuses there. We seem to have plenty of spare time to binge watch an entire season of our favorite show. Yet, when it comes to our responsibilities and striving for our potential, there's no shortage of excuses.

One way to see clearly where we all succumb to this habit of making excuses is with New Year's resolutions. For so many of us, we could simply change the date – and keep all of the same resolutions from one year to the next! Every year we make our list, hoping to change, only to come back 12 months later and start all over again. We may start out strong but our efforts dwindle as the year goes on. We excuse ourselves with statements such as "This is who I am, I just can't change," or "It's too hard to break this habit." Is that really true? Is it really too hard to change? One way to know if something is truly beyond your reach is to ask yourself the following question: If someone were to offer you $100,000 to conquer this resolution once and for all, would you be able to do it? It is amazing how easy something really difficult becomes when our desire kicks in.

Free Will is Power

If we really wanted to be great, all of our excuses would disappear. The simple truth is that we undeniably have the power to accomplish anything we put our minds to. This power comes from a concept which Judaism taught the world – that each of us has free will. Free will is the greatest gift of life. It is the ability for us to choose who we wish to be. We have the power to choose lives filled with meaning and dignity, or choose to escape into a cave of illusion and comfort. The power to change our lives comes with the weight of responsibility, because if I have free will, the only person responsible for me – is me. Free will means I can't blame my family, my society, or my physical limitations for who I am. Free will means that I, and I alone, am responsible for the world I create for myself.

Free will is not simply a matter of choice, the way we might choose chocolate ice cream over vanilla. That is simply a matter of preference. Determinists mistakenly associate these types of choices with free will. On the contrary, free will choices deal specifically with matters that make a difference in who we are as a person. These are the only choices that differentiate us from animals and make us human. A dog also prefers one type of food versus another. However, a dog can't choose to change its character. A dog can never choose to be anything other than a dog. We, on the other hand, can choose to elevate ourselves and build our character, or demean ourselves, sometimes even acting lower than an animal in the process.

Choice of Life or Death

Another mistake often made is that free will is the choice between good and bad. While that may be true in theory, it is not a practical definition. Even evil dictators who commit atrocities and other horrific acts of cruelty believe they are doing so for the good of humanity, their country, or, at the very least, themselves. That is because we always choose what we think is good even when we knowingly make wrong choices. We justify and rationalize for that moment that doing this foolish act is what we need. Therefore, asserting that we have the power to choose good over bad is not very meaningful, because good and bad are relative terms. Instead, the ultimate act of free will is really the choice between life and death. This choice is a constant struggle.

Death is not only the ending of life. There are momentary acts of suicide as well. Wasting time is the most tragic example of this. When we choose to escape our responsibilities and waste time, we are experiencing and indulging in momentary death.

There was a car chase in Los Angeles involving a bank robbery. In an attempt to get rid of the evidence, the criminals were throwing the stolen money out the window as they sped through the streets. Imagine if you saw someone doing this as he casually drove down a highway. Each time the driver would throw money out the window you would probably recklessly try to grab the bills as they flew by your car. If you both ended up pulling into the same convenience store parking lot, imagine the shock you would experience if he asked if you could spare some money for him to buy gas! This fool just threw hundreds of dollars out of his window, and now he has the audacity to ask you for money?! The tragedy of this story is that we would condemn a person for throwing money away, but rarely consider how often we throw our time away. We constantly throw our time out the window. Whether it is simply allowing time to pass by idly or by wasting time escaping from our responsibilities, we casually allow ourselves to spend this valuable commodity on trivialities on a daily basis. That is the real struggle of free will: "To be, or not to be". To embrace our responsibilities and use our time productively, or to give in to complacency, laziness or the whims of our emotions and desires.

Take a Break to Recharge

At the same time, living a life of meaning, purpose and responsibility does not mean living in a constant state of unrelenting toil. Everyone needs a break now and then. If we don't take care of ourselves then we certainly won't be able to take care of anyone else. People all too often burn out as a result of disregarding this necessity. However, there is a vast difference between taking a break and escaping. It is interesting how many times we are less energized after returning from a vacation than we were before we left. That's because there are two kinds of vacation. One is when we take a break in order to come back. The other is where we are looking for a reason to escape our responsibilities but call it a vacation in order to mask the truth. Choosing to live requires that we take the time to reinvigorate and refresh, while continuously trying to minimize the amount of time we attempt to escape and waste time.

Don't be a Zombie

The first step in this process is to train ourselves to simply be aware. We should not merely pass through life like zombies walking the earth. How often do we allow ourselves to go through life on autopilot? The key to not being a zombie is to choose to be fully involved wherever you are at that moment. Do not allow time or circumstances to decide life for you. A popular catchphrase now is "learn to be in the moment." Part of being in the moment is to actively choose to be there. Whatever activity you are doing – do it because you choose to be there.

Don't be a Puppet

The second stage of using our free will is not to rely on choices that were made for us, or on choices we have made in the past. Obviously, allowing others to decide our lives for us is a failure to engage in life. However, even our own choices need to be constantly reexamined. A 30 year-old's understanding of life ought to be more developed than a teenager's. Just because we decided something at an earlier age does not mean it should stay with us forever.

Even those decisions that we do want to remain with us need constant refreshing, otherwise they become stale with time. Periodically we should check our assumptions and make sure they are really what we continue to choose now.

Body Versus Soul

Once we are aware of the struggle of free will, we must then begin to understand the nature of the battle. That battle stems from the disparity between our emotions and our intellect. We all want greatness. Every human being wants to be great. We just don't feel like making the effort. This struggle is the constant conflict between the body and the soul. Our soul yearns for meaning and accomplishment, while the body yearns – just as strongly – for comfort. This desire for comfort will be discussed further in the chapter on perseverance, but for now we can all appreciate that the body just wants a soft couch and a blanket. The soul, on the other hand, derives pleasure from achievement. This can only be attained by taking responsibility.

Responsibility is Pleasure

Responsibility and obligation should not be mistaken for a burden. A burden is something we have no choice but to do, and serves us no benefit. Responsibility, however, is an obligation we must perform because it provides us with pleasure. Sadly, we often incorrectly label our obligations as burdens. For example, when we cease recognizing the benefit and pleasure to be had from our parents, a spouse or a child, they become burdens in our eyes. Once something is deemed a burden the urge to escape it is immense.

One would think that according to religion the greatest pleasure that could be had is to have an existential experience. What greater spiritual experience could there be than to communicate with the Almighty? Judaism, however, takes a different approach. Rather than communing with God, Judaism believes that the greatest pleasure is to be like God.

When Abraham was 99 years old, he was told to circumcise himself. That physical ordeal led to great pain, and God came to visit Abraham and comfort him. Yet, Abraham leaves the presence of God and runs to offer hospitality to what appear to be three vagrants traveling on the road. Imagine if the President of the United States came to visit you in your home. Could you possibly fathom excusing yourself while he was there to go take care of three homeless people begging for change? To us, what Abraham did was incredulous. Yet Abraham understood there is something even more powerful than a personal experience with God. He understood that if he really wanted to experience the pleasure of a relationship with an Infinite Being, then instead of experiencing God, he would need to become like God. Being Godly is taking responsibility for the world.

Every decision we make in life is based on what will give us more pleasure. Regardless of what that decision is, we choose the one we believe will give us more pleasure, either now or in the future. If instead of studying for an exam, we choose to stay up late partying, then we are demonstrating that the momentary pleasure of that evening is worth more to us than the long term effect of failing the test. On the other hand, if we pass on social indulgences, and put in the proper amount of effort, then we are choosing the long-term pleasure of graduating, finding a good job, and the pleasure that will come from that. This approach is true regarding all of our choices in life. The more responsibility that we choose to have in life the more pleasure we will have. The person who saw to it that a hospital is built in the community gets much more pleasure than a staff member in that hospital. Both take responsibility for the lives of the people in the community, but one took greater responsibility, and therefore reaps greater pleasure.

Choosing to change the world is a daunting task, and it may seem like a burden at times. But take a moment to think about what it truly means to change the world for the better. Of course it's a tremendous responsibility – but can there be any greater pleasure than achieving that goal? The more responsibility we take on the more the pleasure we have. No one else is going to do it for us, and no there's no one else to blame if we do not. Take stock of your various responsibilities. Realize that they are not merely responsibilities but obligations. The buck stops with you. Take pleasure that those obligations are yours and no one else's. They are your special treasures to be nurtured and cultivated by you, and the more you do so, the more pleasure they will bring you.

Choose Life

- Being able to do something means you are responsible, and being responsible means your are obligated.
- No one is responsible for your life other than you.
- Make a list of the three aspects about your life you wish to change.
- Identify the excuses you keep making that allow you to push off making that change.
- Ask yourself if you were offered $100,000 to accomplish each one, would those excuses vanish?
- Make a list of all the areas in your life that you are responsible for and spell out how each one enhances your life and gives you pleasure.

THREE

Fear:
Live With The Reality of
Consequences

"Death is very likely the single best invention of life."
Steve Jobs

Along with clarity and the awareness that we have obligations, we must learn to live with something that many people find difficult to accept. We must learn to live with and embrace fear.

I will never forget the first time I saw someone truly terrified. I was leading a three-week trip in Israel for American university students. We took the students on a hike in the northern region of Israel through a breathtaking canyon. At several points along the hike we needed to cross a river by swimming through it. Entry into the river was most often easy. However, there was one point where the river went over a fall and the only way to continue was by climbing down a fifty-foot ladder into the river alongside the fall. Sounds exhilarating – unless you are afraid of heights. We had asked the students before the hike if they could all swim, but mistakenly did not think that we also had to inquire about the fear of heights.

When we reached the ladder one student came over to me and informed me that he was indeed terrified of heights. At this point in the canyon there was really not much we could do unless we wanted to call in for a helicopter to lift him out. I told him I would wait to go down the ladder with him. About three-quarters of the way through our group he mustered up the courage and decided he would make the attempt. It took a few moments for him to maneuver himself onto the ladder. He then paused to gather more strength.

At this point another group of hikers came up behind us. This group was comprised of avid outdoors people so this particular hike was very basic for them. They began to get agitated by the wait. To this day I am shocked at what happened next. The group behind us decided they did not need to wait any longer and actually began to climb over my student.

This was disastrous. He went into a panic. He was screaming for help and shrieking for them to get off of him. They ignored all of our pleas. When they finally finished passing us, I believe my student was in shock. He would not respond. I began to worry we just might need that helicopter.

It was clear the only course would be to physically walk him down the ladder. I told him what we were going to do and then climbed over him. First his right leg was lowered to the next step, then his left. His fingers had to be pried loose from the ladder and each hand lowered. This entire process was repeated until he was about ten feet above the water. At that point he was able to continue on his own. I will most likely never forget witnessing that moment of sheer, paralyzing fear. That is what most people envision when thinking about fear. Certainly not a positive image.

Where Fear Comes From

Most people say that fear comes from the unknown. That is a mistake. My student knew exactly what he was afraid of – falling to his death in the river. Picture yourself on a safari in Africa, enjoying the scenery and the unbelievable photo opportunities, when your guide tells you not to move. Turning around, you spot a huge lion lurking behind your group. The lion begins to charge.

Are you afraid?

Of course.

Why? Do you not know what is going to happen? Of course not! You know exactly what is about to happen, which is exactly why you are afraid!

The truth is that fear does not come from the unknown, rather it comes from the known. It comes from what we perceive to be harmful or dangerous. No one is scared of flying, they are scared of crashing. No one is scared of the ocean, they are scared of drowning or being attacked by sharks. No one is scared of the dark, they are scared of what may be in the dark. The Hebrew word for fear has the same root as that which means to see. Fear comes from seeing reality, an awareness that there are consequences in life.

Little babies who are first learning how to crawl cannot be left alone at the top of the stairs. Why? Because they don't know that they don't have the skill to go down steps yet. Therefore, they are not afraid of falling. Their parents might be – but they certainly are not. Baby animals, on the other hand, will not go down a set of stairs. I remember as a child that my family's puppy would go upstairs while we went out but would be stuck there when we came home. He knew how to go up the steps but was terrified to come down.

Any one of us who has played trust games knows that if you trust the person you are teamed with there is nothing to fear. If your husband or wife tells you to close your eyes and they lead you into a room, hopefully you would not be afraid. Yet, if we were to walk into a dark room on our own, we'd have reason to be cautious. It's not simply that we don't know what is in there. Rather, it is because of what we presume to be in there that we are scared. The reason we feel any fear, whether from a known situation or an unknown situation, is that we foresee a negative outcome. Foreseen consequences, or more accurately, foreseen negative consequences, is the basis of all fears. When there are no perceived negative consequences, there is nothing to fear.

Many people who have been involved in a bad relationship or suffered through a loveless marriage have an overwhelming fear of marriage. They will choose to live with someone for years, sometimes for the remainder of their life, rather than marry. They fear that what they have seen or experienced in marriage will happen to them. Again, this is based on an assumption that the only outcome to a marriage is negative. For some reason, the possibility that a marriage could work, or that they have the power and choice to make it work, does not occur to them as an option.

The Fear of Dying

One of the things that people fear most is death. This too fits into our definition of fear. For those who believe there is nothing after death the fear is quite simple. There can be no greater negative outcome than for everything to just end. If there is nothing after this life then our existence ceases. That can be quite frightening. For those who believe there is some type of existence after this life, then the fear usually stems from concern over receiving a negative judgment. Either way, the greatest fear of death is the prospect that I will not have achieved all that I wanted to in this life.

This final fear is the only one we should embrace. Rather than fearing death, better we should fear what we do or don't do while we are alive. If we fail to make the most out of this life, then we must face the consequences that come with that choice. If we, on the other hand, choose to live life to the best of our ability, we have nothing to fear. The student who earnestly studies for the exam can take the test with a good conscience regardless of what grade is received.

This is why truly wise people have never feared death throughout the ages. In every generation there have been righteous people that have been forced to choose between their values and death and have valiantly chosen death. Such people harbor no perceived negative outcome

after this life. The only fear that a wise person does have is
that death will be an inability to accomplish more in this
world. That is the only thing we should fear. Fear should be a
motivator to live more, to grow more and to accomplish
more. Every day we should wake up and be afraid of what
we might not accomplish if we don't make the most of that
day.

Fear is Motivational

Fear is a tremendous tool if we choose to face it.
One day we will no longer have the opportunity that this life
gives us. That fear should motivate each one of us to do the
most we can while we are alive. That realization is what fear
is all about, that there are consequences in this life. In fact,
fear is the catalyst for our free will.   Anytime we do
something it is either because we are choosing to accept fear
or we are choosing to hide from fear. Judaism says that the
very first step to wisdom is fear. Becoming a wise person is
a consequence of perceiving the outcome and acting upon it.
In other words, learning to embrace and live with fear.

The Negative View of Fear

The notion that we should embrace fear seems to be
counterintuitive. After all, who wants to go through life
looking over his shoulder? If you recall the image of my
student clutching to the ladder for dear life, that is not an
image any of us would call enticing. The most basic reason
fear has a negative association is that it has the potential to

make us feel debilitated, unable to act or respond, like a frightened mouse cowering in the corner. As we discussed in the previous chapter, every decision we make is for pleasure. Living with fear does not rank very high on the list of pleasures available to us. Additionally, the notion of being constantly afraid is somewhat belittling. Why, then, should fear be one of the crucial traits in becoming a man?

Fear is Desirable

In truth, there are two types of fear. One type of fear is the embodiment of all those negative effects, while the other is a powerful tool for life. For example, almost every one of us has at one point or another paid money to be scared. Whether it was for a roller coaster or haunted house at an amusement park, or whether we bought a movie ticket to watch a horror film, the prospect of being scared was a thrill. Fear reminds us that we are alive and that it is a thrill to be alive.

Going a step further, fear can actually motivate and empower us to accomplish great things. There are numerous stories that can be found easily on the internet of individuals performing tremendous feats of strength while in a state of total fear. The 20 year-old woman who lifted the car off of her father, or the teenager who lifted the car off of his grandfather both were able to do so out of fear of what was going to happen to their loved one. Many soldiers have written about the experience of being in a battle. In the anticipation of the strike there is incredible trepidation, but when the moment of real fear comes and when the alarm goes off, what most do is spring into immediate action. 'Move, move, move!' Fear is a catalyst for action. The expression "get some fire under your feet" is precisely that notion. Fire! Get moving!

Fear of Inadequacy

However, there is a fear that is negative, namely, the fear of failure due to our own inadequacy. It is a fear we should avoid at all costs. The worst outlook to have in life is to view ourselves as inadequate. Often, the times when we do not stand up to fear are precisely those times when we are worried that we will be inadequate to the task. At such times, we mistakenly assume that whatever obstacles are in our way are insurmountable. Since we won't be able to handle the situation anyway, we just avoid the fear by avoiding the situation.

The irony is that running from fear is counter productive for our pleasure. It is precisely the times when we stand up and face our fears, challenge the bully (perhaps even getting a black eye in the process) that we remember with such pleasure down the road. Contrast this to whenever we gave in to our fear of inadequacy, and we will quickly see how different the two experiences can be. When we live with the remorse of our inadequacy, we feel like a failure. Allowing ourselves to become paralyzed by fear sows the seeds of regret from that moment onward.

Like my student on the ladder, I also had a moment of paralyzing fear. In the summer after my freshman year in high school I was on a trip to Niagara Falls, Canada. Three of my friends and I decided to explore a local indoor shopping center. While we were in there we passed a haunted house. A haunted house in the middle of a mall? Whoever heard of such a thing? This must surely be a joke. Besides the long line of people waiting to get in, what we found even more ridiculous was the look of sheer horror on those coming out of the exit curtain. We laughed at the notion of being that scared and thought that we would show these tourists how to go through this unscathed. We had no idea what we were in for.

We paid our entrance fee and entered. After we walked down a long corridor we turned a corner and entered extreme darkness. The only thing we could see was a small dot of red light in the distance. That was the haunted house; a maze in total darkness that we were guided through by way of a small red dot of light. Sometimes the dot was a diversion. Sometimes we would walk right into a wall that apparently had a mirror on it showing us the light that was really around a corner. Slowly we began to lose our confidence in our footing. Then came fear. Out of the darkness would come a hand that would touch one of us on the ear. Suddenly a person breathed on one of our necks. Abruptly the sound of a chain would rattle on the floor. Eventually sheer terror took over.

At one point we stopped moving forward altogether. We were too scared of what was going to come out of the darkness next. No one wanted to be the one to go first. We began throwing each other in the front, one after the other, none of us would budge.

It seemed like we were in that spot for hours even though it was probably only minutes. Eventually the staff realized we were not going to move and our first blow to our ego transpired. Over an intercom a calm professional voice came on and said we must continue to move forward as others were waiting to enter the attraction. We were humbled to say the least. Although the reality that this was nothing more than a thrill experience and there was nothing to fear became so apparent at that moment, there was still a slight level of trepidation. That, combined with the affront to our ego, was not a good combination. We were about to be humbled again and this time actually belittled.

The staff continued to torment us as we slowly continued through the maze. However, the next time the chain was rattled on the floor, one of my friends grabbed the chain.

"I've got him!" he yelled.

Then we all grabbed him as well. We were not going to be beat by this. Yet the truth is we were already beaten. Again the voice came on the loudspeaker. This time the tone was stern and serious.

"If you do not let go immediately and move steadily through, we will have to stop the experience and turn on the lights."

At that moment, all fear was removed. The realization that not only was this just a thrill experience but that we had been beaten by it was undeniable. We had brazenly declared that this would not get the better of us. The truth is that it did – and it brought out the worst of us. We were unprepared for what was going to transpire in that maze and therefore we were taken by surprise. We had been inadequate. We did not think that we could go on and handle whatever was going to come our way. That is the fear that is destructive.

Fear of Rejection

That same insecurity and fear prevents us from being ourselves. So many of us go around pretending to be someone we are not, simply out of fear that our true self will be rejected by the people around us. Often, we have an image of who we believe we should or should not be, and we feel inadequate when we compare ourselves to that image. Some men would rather not ask someone on a date or go for a job interview than expose themselves to the possibility of being turned down. To avoid these various forms of rejection we create a protective bubble around ourselves. In some instances, people create a false personality that they hope will be more accepted by the crowd. Others build a wall of isolation around themselves, never allowing any part of themselves to be exposed. Either way their true self becomes buried and lost as a result of this fear.

Using the Power of Fear

So there are really two kinds of fear: one that we should embrace and one that is destructive. The realization that life has serious repercussions and consequences is a fact that we are well aware of. We all know that we must live with the choices we make. Yet, even though we all know that there are consequences in life, we never cease to be shocked by them. The greatest example of this is death itself. No matter what the circumstances are, we always seem to be somewhat shocked when someone dies. It is almost as if we expect people to live forever. This same sense of denial leads us to think that we have all the time in the world. Sure we know we are going to die, someday, just not any time soon. Yet the reality is quite the opposite. No one knows when. We try to deny this reality all the time. We know this inevitability will come and yet we are shocked when it happens. This allows us to go on living with our head in the sand. It allows us to push off our responsibilities by convincing ourselves that we have plenty of time.

The greatest way to be aware that there are consequences in life and to live with that reality is to focus on both possible outcomes in every situation. One of the reasons we don't associate fear with a positive image is that we only picture the negative consequences. Realize that there are positive consequences as well. If you recall the example used in the previous chapter; imagine if someone were to offer you a huge reward to accomplish a task you previously thought was impossible. Suddenly, the obstacles and excuses seem to disappear, or at the very least not seem as big, because we have become laser focused on the reward. Ask a teenager to wake up bright and early on a school day and they will barrage you with a litany of reasons why they can't. Offer them free use of the car on the weekend if they wake up on time all week and they will be singing morning tunes at the breakfast table.

The same logic applies when it comes to our responsibilities. In place of a financial reward, picture the positive results of overcoming our negative fears. If we take our responsibilities seriously, imagine what our lives would be like. The chance to realize those positive results is a tremendous motivator to accomplish. The opposite is also true. Envisioning negative consequences can be an incredible motivator as well. Imagine that same task, only in this instance, the cost of not accomplishing it would be to lose a substantial amount of money. There is no greater loss than the loss of opportunity. The wasted time of our lives is something that can never be replaced.

To truly embrace this power we should ask ourselves profound questions beginning with two simple words: "what if?"

What if you were told you had five years to live? What would you do? How are you going to live your life?

How many years do we have to live?   We don't know.

We don't have to wait until the doctor says we have five years to realize the fragile nature of life. We can ask ourselves that right now. What would I really worry about if I only had five years to live? What do I fear I will not have accomplished by then? What questions would I want answered? What am I living for? What am I doing with my time?

Once those questions are answered, backtrack and ask what if I only have a year? What would I do?

What if I only had three months? What would I do?

Now ask yourself what if I only had one day?

Don't start with one day – it's too difficult to grapple with and come up with a substantial response. But you can start with five years. And once you answer five years, you can continue to ask with less time.

What if today was my last day? Do you want your last day to be the day that you slept in late?

Judaism says we should live every day as if it is the day before we die. If we viewed every day that way, each day would become quite profound.

What if today was the last day?

That's scary!

True – but this can be a positive fear. It can be exhilarating. It can be motivating. I better accomplish a lot today! I have so much to do before it is too late. That is why fear is the ultimate motivator.

Therefore, in addition to having clarity and accepting that we have obligations, we must see that life is fraught with consequences. There will be serious, negative ramifications for our life if we avoid those responsibilities. On the other hand, life will be richly rewarding if we conquer our fears and embrace the task at hand.

Learn to Love Fear

- We only fear what we perceive.
- Fear can be pleasurable.
- Fear is a good thing to have. It prevents us from unnecessary harm and destruction.
- Fear can be negative. It can prevent us from living life to the fullest.
- The worst fear to have is a fear of failure from viewing ourselves as inadequate.
- When in your life have you succumbed to this unhealthy fear?
- Fear can be powerful if it is used to accomplish.
- Make a list of the things you fear most that you might not achieve in life.
- If you knew you only had five years left how would that affect your life?
- Ask yourself every day, "What if this was my last day, would I act differently?"

FOUR

Optimism: Everything That Happens Is For The Best

"Optimism is the faith that leads to achievement. Nothing can be done without hope and confidence."
Helen Keller

Now that we understand the motivational benefits of fear, we must also have the confidence necessary to know that we can absolutely change our world. That confidence comes from optimism. Golda Meir, the first female Prime Minister of Israel, used to say, "Pessimism is a luxury that a Jew can never allow!" Why did she refer to pessimism as a luxury? It seems to be a peculiar word to use. The reason is that pessimism leads to laziness. A pessimist rarely accomplishes anything.

Why? Because a pessimist constantly says, "It can't be done!"

"It won't work."

"Don't bother."

As Helen Keller said, "No pessimist ever discovered the secrets of the stars or sailed to an uncharted land or opened the new heavens to the human spirit." The essence of a pessimist is to not try. How many great ideas or phenomenal undertakings have we thought about accomplishing in our life but did not do so simply because the first thought that came to our mind was, "Don't. Don't bother, it's not going to work"? Why bother when we have convinced ourselves it will be a failure?

This is the attitude of the naysayer. Being a naysayer is just an excuse to do nothing. That is why Golda Meir referred to pessimism as a luxury. However, when surrounded by so many enemies of the Jewish People, with their constant attempts to wipe us out, doing nothing is not even a luxury – it is not even an option.

Pessimism Versus Optimism

The root of pessimism is not just laziness. It also comes from the conviction that nothing can change – a direct contradiction to the very notion of changing our world. A pessimist quits easily because he is convinced nothing can change. Yet, this is not necessarily true. We can learn to be optimistic. If pessimism is the conviction that things are permanent, then optimism is the determination that things are, in fact, open to change. Not only can the circumstances of life change, but a person's character and outlook on life can change as well. Don't ever think that you are the way you are and there is nothing you can do about it. We can change. A person can learn to be optimistic. A person can learn to have a positive outlook on life, and that is the essence of optimism.

An Optimist is the True Realist

Pessimism also leads to cynicism. Most cynics I know always seem to call themselves realists. The truth is that a cynic is nothing more than a glorified pessimist with an acerbic twist. I have found in my experience there are generally two types of cynics. The first is cynical about life in general. They are fond of saying things such as "What difference does it make, you always lose in the end." The second is cynical about people. They are convinced that people can't be trusted. "Everybody is out to get you." "People just care about themselves." I theorize that the root of their cynicism is a direct outgrowth of their unwillingness to see that change truly is possible. The person who is cynical regarding people is someone who might have tried to change himself and his world, but failed. He became frustrated and disillusioned with people and gave up, resulting in a pessimistic view of humanity. On the other side of the coin is the person who is cynical about life. This is someone who is most likely surrounded by people who try to make a difference in themselves and the world while he chooses to remain static. As a defensive coping mechanism, he lashes out and attacks their motives and efforts by saying that their efforts are useless, since nothing will change. Both cynics see change as impossible. A true realist would focus on the fact that change is always possible. That attitude requires cultivation.

Cultivate Good Habits

Human beings are creatures of habit. Almost everything we do is built around habits that we have developed over the course of our lives. Most often when we think of habits we immediately have bad associations, such as biting our nails, overeating, etc. However, there are good habits as well. When we were children, our parents tried to instill good habits in us such as brushing our teeth, saying thank you, etc. We should continue to seek out good habits and constantly go about building them into our character. One such habit is not being negative and pessimistic. Instead, learn to look at the world through the eyes of optimism.

The dictionary defines optimists as those who see the world as a benevolent place. This is the philosophical opposite of pessimism.

Optimists generally believe that people and events are inherently good so that most situations can and will work out for the best in the end. The essence of optimism is a view that things can change for the better. Things will change and ultimately, the very scenario that we are in – even if it appears bad – is ultimately for good as well. Pessimists have the exact opposite view.

Always View the Cup as Half Full

One of the greatest Jewish leaders of all time, Rabbi Akiva, lived during the era of the Roman Empire. In addition to being a great leader, Rabbi Akiva was also a tremendous optimist. His favorite maxim was "whatever happens is always for the best."

Rabbi Akiva lived in the decades following the destruction of the Temple. One time, he and three other rabbis visited the place where the Temple had stood in Jerusalem and saw a fox running through the ruins. To put this in a frame of reference for today, imagine having visited ground zero in Manhattan shortly after 9/11 and seeing rats rummage through the rubble. That would be painful to any American. That is how painful that image must have been to those Rabbis. The symbol of all that was good and holy to the Jewish people lay before them in a heap of ruins. Upon seeing this scene, Rabbi Akiva's colleagues began to weep. Rabbi Akiva, on the other hand, was visibly happy and in fact even laughed. The other rabbis were shocked. How could he witness such great destruction and laugh?

"Don't you see what is happening over there?" he replied. "There is a fox running through the ruins. A prophecy was foretold to the Jewish people before the destruction that the Temple would lie in ruins but would be rebuilt one day." Rabbi Akiva was teaching them that now that this prophecy of destruction had happened, so to the other prophecy regarding the rebuilding of the Temple will happen as well. Jerusalem will one day be rebuilt.

Rabbi Akiva had the ability, to focus on the fact that even though the destruction was painful and real, it would only be temporary. He told them that the pain they were experiencing will end and that there will once again be time for rejoicing. The other rabbis were comforted by his words. His optimism prevailed.

Another incident demonstrating Rabbi Akiva's optimism occurred when he arrived at a city one night after the gates had closed and was forced to sleep in the forest outside the gates. A lion came in the middle of the night and ate his donkey. Rabbi Akiva did not lament but rather remarked that it must be for the good. A cat then ate his rooster and Rabbi Akiva again said, "it's for the good." A wind subsequently blew out his candle. Again Rabbi Akiva said, "it's for the good."

The next morning, he found out that a group of marauders had destroyed the town and carried off the inhabitants into captivity. If his donkey, rooster or candle had been there, he would have been noticed and would have been taken as well. The candles were blown out, so no one saw him. The rooster was taken, so nobody heard him. Despite being locked out of the city, in the end it turned out for the best.

In both stories it would have been understandable for Rabbi Akiva to have gotten caught up in the loss and disappointment of the moment. Instead, Rabbi Akiva had the ability to see beyond the details of the moment to the underlying truth that if God is running the world, everything that happens must be for the good.

Similarly, Rabbi Akiva's triumphant rise to greatness is an unbelievable story of dedication and conviction that could only have happened through optimism. He did not start out with the resources or knowledge that normally allow people to achieve greatness. Before he became one of the most famous educators and leaders of the Jewish people, Rabbi Akiva lived the first 40 years of his life as an ignorant and uneducated person!

Not only was he uneducated but he was extremely skeptical of those who were. He used to say, "Show me a Rabbi and I will bite him like a donkey." He would walk around saying, "Why should I even bother associating myself with these Rabbis? All they do is look down upon me. All they do is judge me. All they do is think negatively of me." He had no ability to see that there could be anything positive whatsoever to be gained from Rabbis. In short, he lived the first 40 years of his life as a pessimist with regard to this issue.

Yet, when he was 40 years old, Rabbi Akiva managed to pick himself up and go study for 24 years. That means all the great accomplishments we know about Rabbi Akiva did not even begin to happen until he was 64 years old! Could you imagine what he must have gone through when he began? There was no adult education back then, which means that he must have gone to a class filled with children. Just imagine the ridicule he must have endured. How was he able to withstand that humiliation? Dwight D. Eisenhower said, "Pessimism never won any battle." Where did Rabbi Akiva get the optimism needed to fight this battle?

He received it from his wife, Rachel. Rachel was the daughter of the wealthiest man alive at the time, and Rabbi Akiva was a stablehand on their ranch. Rachel saw that this man had tremendous potential. She kept telling him that he had tremendous potential, and could be great one day. Every one of us can be great. Imagine if we had someone behind us telling us that all the time?

"You could be great!"

Rabbi Akiva had Rachel telling him this.

Her father found out about their relationship and he told her, "If you continue this relationship you are cut off! You will never see a dime of my money! Nothing!"

Rachel went to Rabbi Akiva and told him that regardless of that threat she was willing to marry him and forgo all that money on one condition – that Rabbi Akiva go and learn in order to achieve his potential. He agreed. He went from sheer negativity to having open possibilities. How?   Because he had someone standing behind him, saying, "I have confidence in you! I love you, and I know that you can do it."

He ended up learning for 24 years. After all that time, he returned home with 24,000 students. Upon arriving in his hometown, Rachel came out to greet him. Rabbi Akiva's students had no idea who this woman was. Imagine walking up to a famous person with all the entourage and trying to get close to say hello. So the students blocked her way, until Rabbi Akiva saw her and told them to let her through, because whatever they think they have, it belongs to her.   He would have been nothing without her. Rachel is what gave Rabbi Akiva the confidence.

Being Loved Leads to Self-Respect

Knowing that we are loved is one of the most crucial elements of human existence. Every one of us needs to know that we are special and unique in our own way. That tremendous sense of self-worth is what gives us confidence and security. It is such a vital ingredient for success in life that Jewish law mandates that we view ourselves as good people. The ability to view ourselves this way comes from a realization that we are loved. The Hebrew word for mother connotes that a mother is the first person that gives a child a sense of belief. This cannot mean that she gives her infant child or toddler a belief in an Infinite Being. Rather, it means that the nurturing and love the mother showers upon her children is what allows them to believe in themselves, to believe they are special because they are loved.

It is no accident that Rabbi Akiva not only taught that "everything that happens is for the best," but also that human beings are loved by God. Rabbi Akiva famously said the following: "Beloved is humanity." Life is all about perspective. As John F. Kennedy said, "You know people are complaining about the 20 percent unemployment, but just remember 20 percent unemployment means that there are 80 percent that are employed." It is all how we choose to look at it. That is why an optimist thinks that this world is awesome and this is the way it is supposed to be, whereas the pessimist assumes that the current situation can never improve – and if anything will only get worse. It is all based on their perspective. As Harry Truman said, "A pessimist is one who makes difficulties of his opportunities, an optimist is one who makes opportunities from his difficulties." What greater perspective can a person have than to live with the awareness that they are special, because God loves them?

Not too long ago I was in an airport and I saw this little boy, about the age of five, wearing a t-shirt that said, "I know I'm not junk because God doesn't make junk." Imagine if your father was a billionaire. The world could not possibly intimidate you unless you felt some sense of insecurity in yourself. Imagine if the Creator of the Universe loved you specifically. To live with that would be to live with a tremendous sense of confidence and optimism.

Seven Steps to Building Optimism

There are seven steps to develop that kind of optimism. Step one is to acknowledge that God loves you. The very fact that we are alive means God loves us. None of us had to be born. The very fact that we were born means that God loves us. The Almighty thought that it was necessary for us to be in the world. How would it feel if upon arriving home after being away there was a billboard at your airport welcoming you back personally?

"Shalom Denbo, welcome back, we missed you. Signed, the City of Los Angeles."

The feeling of exhilaration and love would be immense. Every morning we should view the world as a massive billboard welcoming us back with a statement saying, "Welcome back to My universe, signed God."

Step two is to understand that even though our parents love us, they are not always aware of who we truly are. How many parents have any idea of what their children's dreams and aspirations are? Most parents are not fully aware of their children. To many parents, their children are strangers to them. Some have the lucky opportunity to actually have a close relationship, but even those who do, do not truly know what is in the hearts of their children. God, on the other hand, is totally aware of everything we could possibly want as well as everything we should want.

Step three is to know that there is nothing that we could possibly want that the Almighty does not have the power to give us. Name something God cannot do. Nothing is impossible for God. He has the power to do anything and everything. Interestingly, the Talmud states that matching the right man with the right woman is as difficult for the Almighty as splitting the sea. The notion that anything is difficult for the Almighty is absurd. Splitting the sea was nothing more than a cessation of the laws of nature, which are only laws because God created them. As such, splitting the sea was no more difficult for God than us tying our shoes. The comparison to finding a soulmate is meant to convey the understanding that feats that we find so daunting, such as finding the right person to marry, building a business, raising children, and changing the world, are nothing to the Almighty. God can make them happen as easily as he split the sea.

The fourth step is to get rid of the ego. Realize that I can't do it myself. I need help. Anything I wish to accomplish in life requires assistance from others. Nothing can be done entirely on our own. Even something as relatively simple as painting a portrait requires the involvement of many other people. Someone had to supply the paint, another the brushes and the canvas, and someone else had to teach us how to paint. Everything we do is dependent on the involvement of others. This step will be discussed further in the chapter on unity.

Step five is to remember that God has a track record. Children often ask their parents for absurd requests, only to be shocked when the response is no. That is because they expect the answer to be yes as a result of the parent having built a track record of giving. The same is true for the Almighty. He has a track record of having given us a tremendous amount of good. How many times have we asked for things, gotten them, and then forgot about it? All we have to do is think back on our lives and see how many times we have been in a jam.   How many times have we been in a situation that we thought would never work out? How many times were we unable to see anything good about the situation and yet, when we jump forward in life we can see it was a good thing? It was a good thing that they fired me from that company, because now I have this job over here. It was a good thing that she broke up with me, because now I finally met this girl. It was a good thing that such and such happened, because that created the opening for something else. You want to know God loves you? Simply look back at the fact that God has a tremendous track record of doing amazing things in your life.

Step six is to be aware that we don't have to "deserve" anything. What did we do to deserve our eyes? What did we do to deserve legs? What did we do to deserve the ability to think or the ability to speak? What did we do to deserve any of these gifts? We didn't do anything! We got these gifts without deserving them.

Anyone who is a parent knows that is the way we should deal with our children. No parent should give necessary things to their children or take such things away because they deserve it. We should give to our children because we love our children. We should give because our children need it. Period!

Can you imagine an emotionally healthy parent saying to their child, "You are not getting dinner tonight, you don't deserve it"? Nonsense. "I am not taking you to school, you don't deserve it." Absurd.

We don't deal with children that way. We give to them because we love them, not because they deserve it. We did not receive the gift of life because we deserved it. Therefore, receiving anything I could possibly ask for or achieving anything I could possibly wish to accomplish, has nothing to do with whether I deserve it or not. One of the most prevalent reasons why we become naysayers and turn into pessimists is that we think that we don't deserve our life to be any better. This is my lot in life because this is what I deserve. That is nonsense. We didn't do anything to deserve the ability to think and yet we can. Is there anything that you want to accomplish in this life that is greater than the ability to think? And yet we were given that. Don't dismiss your optimism based on what you think you don't deserve.

For many readers, it is the seventh step that presents the most difficulty, because it is the one step we would rather not hear. Until now the messages have been easy to swallow. God loves me. God is aware of what I want and what I desire. God has the power, rather than myself. God has given me so much in the past, so there is no reason to think He is not going to give me now. I have never deserved anything in the past, so there is no reason to think I need to deserve it now. Therefore, I have every reason to think that He will continue to give me what I want. Step seven delivers a dose of reality.

The final step is to understand that God knows what is best for us. The reason we don't like to hear this is that we honestly believe that if something does not work out the way we want, it cannot be good. The same expectation that causes a child to ask for a ridiculous toy is what causes his incredible disappointment and often resentment towards his parents when the answer is no. However, as the adult, the parent has the responsibility to determine if what the child is asking for is actually in his best interest. Most children are unable to see this. Most children only see that they did not get what they wanted. That is why the Rabbis with Rabbi Akiva looked at the destruction and cried. They could not see how the destruction was good for the Jewish people. Yet, Rabbi Akiva was able to comfort them by showing them a different perspective.

The Ultimate View of Optimism

Adolescents are able to discern some areas in which it is beneficial for them to act and some that are not. However, even though they have some level of discernment, that does not mean they should be given total jurisdiction over all their decisions. Would you allow a 14 year-old to decide whether to drop out of school? Would you allow a 14 year-old to decide to get married? Would you allow a 14 year-old to move out of the house and hike across the country? Of course not. They could easily argue (and probably would) that they "need" to experience the world. But the parent must be able to say, "You are fourteen, but I am the parent and I know better. As a parent I have a broader scope than you have." So too, God has a broader scope than we have. Like teenagers trying to protect their ego, we don't like to hear that anyone knows better – even if that someone is God.

Rabbi Akiva is trying to teach us that if we are aware that we are loved, whatever is in our best interest will happen. We can be optimistic. With that we can go back to the definition of optimism that the dictionary gave us and understand it a bit deeper. Optimism is not that everything will work out the way I want it to. That is fantasy. Rather, optimism is an outlook on life that views the world as a positive place or one's personal situation as positive. Regardless of the circumstances at the moment, life is positive, period. If God loves me it is not possible that something that is happening to me is bad. I may not be able to perceive it as good, but I can be secure in the knowledge that since it is coming from a benevolent God, it cannot be bad.   Genuine optimism can only be found in a person who understands that there is a benevolent Infinite being. Without that understanding, it is impossible to be a true optimist. Otherwise, everything is nothing more than random chance.   How can "chance" change for the better? By definition random chance or determinism mandates that the world is what it is and there is nothing we can do about it. It might change just by the course of natural physics, but if you study natural physics, you will find that the course of natural physics is that everything changes for the worse. Things deteriorate, rather than getting better. It is only when a person has an understanding that there is an Infinite Being who loves us and wants our good, that we can be truly optimistic. It is with that optimism that we can choose to affect the world and make it better. That must be what ultimately is for the best. Therefore when we decide how we are going to change our world we can and must have the confidence to know that it can be done. Regardless of whether the outcome is what we had hoped for or not, the change that took place was absolutely for our benefit.

Learn to be Optimistic

- Pessimism is an excuse to do nothing.
- Pessimism can lead to cynicism.
- Identify areas in life where you are pessimistic.
- How has that pessimism hurt you?
- Optimism is knowing that the world is good and can only get better.
- Every day say the following: "God loves me!"
- Every day go over the 7 steps:
    1. God loves me.
    2. God knows all my desires.
    3. God has the power to deliver whatever it is I am asking for.
    4. I don't have the power to do this on my own.
    5. God has a track record so I can expect it.
    6. I don't even have to deserve it so there is no reason to think that it won't happen.
    7. God knows what is best and therefore even if I don't receive what I am asking for it must be for the best.

FIVE

Joy:
See The Potential

"Everything is amazing right now and nobody's happy."
Louis C.K.

Once we have clarity of our goals, combined with a real sense of obligation and consequence, as well as the confidence that we can make a difference, the next ingredient is the energy and motivation that comes from joy. Joy fills us with an infectious energy. The natural state of a human being is to be filled with joy. You may find that hard to believe. After all, look at so many of the people around us. How many appear to be living with joy? Not too many. It never ceases to amaze me when I look at the expressions on people's faces how angry the world seems. Especially when they're driving! Based on the look on their faces, it is a wonder that most of these people don't just throw in the towel. They look miserable! Nevertheless, that is not the natural state of a person nor how we should be.

When my wife and I first moved to California we had only one daughter at the time. We were living in a townhouse complex in Santa Monica and ours was the fourth unit in from the front gate. The distance from our door to the gate was probably about 75 feet. Most of the time it would take our daughter, who was a year and a half at the time, at least ten to twenty minutes to walk that distance. Every step of the way, she found some new fascination. She would be mesmerized by a crack in the pavement, a flower, or even a solitary ant. When she would finally be coaxed into moving on from that spot, a new fixation would immediately capture her attention. That fascination with life is the natural state of existence.

Each one of us was the same way when we were toddlers. We had an insatiable desire to know everything there was to know in the world. The one question that could never be asked enough was "why?" For every answer our mother gave us about some insight into the deep understandings of the universe, such as why is rain wet, we immediately followed up with "but why is it made out of water?" Life was thrilling and we wanted as much of it as we could get. The thought of going to bed and missing out on something or ending whatever we were engaged in at the time was the greatest torture, an evil decree meted out by our parents.

We have Learned to be Miserable

Why don't we live with the same state of joy we had as children? The answer is that we have learned to be miserable! We have learned to expect disappointment! Every now and then we get a glimpse of it again. If you would like to see this in person, the next time you are at an amusement park watch people as they walk away after exiting a roller coaster ride. They are giddy with laughter! Ecstatic just to be alive! At least at first. However, it isn't too long before the euphoria fades and the energy dies down, and they are back to grumbling about the long lines or how much the soda costs at the snack stand. Just moments ago they were filled with energy and the realization of how great it is to be alive, and now the misery of existence has returned. We do this on a constant basis. We lose focus. We forget the sheer joy of just being alive. It begins with the childish sense of misery when our parents say no to the toy or the extra dessert. Later on, when we experience real disappointment, we forget how to rebound and begin to associate our lives as brief moments of pleasure and joy separated by far too many experiences of disappointment and pain.

Without Joy There is No Desire to Live

This attitude towards life is destructive. The reason for this is that joy is the fuel for life. Joy gives us the energy to tackle the great responsibilities and tests that come our way. Without joy, we have no motivation. Without joy, we are stagnant.

The story of Cain and Abel is a powerful reminder of this reality. Everyone is familiar with Cain's famous statement, "Am I my brother's keeper?" in which he sought to hide the fact that he had just killed his brother. However, the events that led to this tragedy shed light on the importance of living with a sense of joy. In truth, Cain was the first manipulator in history. He thought that if he threw the Almighty a bone in the form of a sacrificial offering, then God would respond with great blessings. The problem was that Cain was focused only on what he would receive in return for his "sacrifice." He did not really want to give up anything – and certainly none of his hard-earned produce. Therefore, his offering was nothing more than a few remnants of his crops.

Abel, on the other hand, had no ego. Abel saw a good idea and implemented it. He also gave an offering. He didn't care that he wasn't the one who came up with it. Even though he was following Cain's lead in bringing an offering, Abel did so out of a pure heart. His offering was brought from the best of his flocks. Naturally God accepted Abel's offering and refused Cain's, and so Cain became distraught. Seeing this, God asked Cain why he was so downcast. He told Cain that wallowing in self-pity would not change anything. Instead, God told Cain that the formula was very simple. All he had to do was work on improving himself. Taking that simple step would lead him to a life of energy and joy. However, if he did not improve, then it would inevitably lead to a pattern of negativity that would become ingrained in his personality and ultimately destroy his life.

Sadness and depression are counter-productive. They keep us from moving forward and do nothing but harm to our character. If a person constantly says, "This is not going to work," or "Why me, why did this have to happen?" then he will never make progress. Joy is the only thing that gives a person the impetus and ability to move on to the next stage of life. When we have joy we jump out of bed. Without it we just want to hit the snooze button through life.

To regain our sense of joy, we first need to understand where it comes from. Joy is the emotional state of being in which one is entirely happy and expresses and exudes pleasure.

When I ask people to describe when a person would most likely express an explosion of joy, the most common answer is winning the lottery. The second most common answer is when a sports team wins a significant game. These are classic moments when we see an explosion of joy.

In Jewish thought, there are actually three main categories of joy, each with its own subtle differences and characteristics: For the purposes of our discussion, we will refer to them as delusional joy, illusionary joy and substantive joy.

False Sense of Joy

As the term implies, delusional joy is experienced when we convince ourselves that something is true, when in reality there is no truth behind the emotion. It is all imaginary. While this may upset many readers, the classic example of this is when our team wins the big game. Part of that joy is delusional. I am not saying that there is nothing joyous or pleasurable about the experience. There is something very powerful and joyous about watching our team win. We will discuss what that is later in this chapter. However, a significant part of that joy is delusional, because it is based on a false sense of accomplishment. We delude ourselves into thinking that simply by identifying with a certain team, we actually share in their achievements. It may be true that since the athletes know their fans are cheering them on they perform better. That allows us as fans to share in the joy of their achievement. But it's important to remember that we did not actually do anything. Additionally, many people believe that because their team won the championship, life in their city will somehow be amazing. Last I checked, though, winning the Super Bowl or World Series had little effect on the long-term crime rate in the winning team's city. Once the celebrations die down, life remains the same.

Another example of this joy is when a fictional character from a movie or TV show we identify with triumphs over a challenge. The tears of joy we shed are very real even though the events are purely imaginary.

Next is illusionary joy. This type of joy has some truth to it, but it is not entirely real. Magicians are illusionists. What they are showing us is real, but what we see is not the full picture. Everything we see is real, but something is amiss. The joy we would experience at winning the lottery is an illusionary sense of joy. What is the illusion? That my life has forever changed for the better. The money is real – but the illusion is that it is automatically for the better. It is very similar to the joy a teenager experiences when he buys his first car. The car brings freedom to go wherever he wants. His parents, on the other hand, see things a bit differently. Yes, there is some truth there, some freedom. However, without limits and responsibility, the end result could be harmful or worse. The illusion is that I am free because I have a car, or because I have all the money I could ever need.   The reality is that these things are no more helpful to me than my ability to handle them properly.

Anticipate the Pleasure

In every instance of joy, whether real or not, the common denominator is the expectation of new possibilities. I got married so I am filled with joy. Why? Look at how wonderful my life will be. I got a raise, now what? Look at all the stuff I can afford! Someone who I haven't seen in a long time came back from a trip. What is the joy? Now I get to spend time with them. We designed a product. Now we can sell it! Every aspect of joy is filled with the anticipation of good things to come. That is the source of joy.

Consider this for a moment. Can there be any greater joy than the anticipation of life? Of waking up in the morning, and seeing what the day will bring? The countless possibilities that await us simply by being alive? Why don't we see that? What is the problem that prevents us from having that perspective? In a word, we get distracted. We forget to focus on what we can do and instead focus on what we can't do. The first aspect of joy is learning to anticipate the pleasure. That is why toddlers have so much joy; they see opportunities for pleasure all the time. If we learn to anticipate the pleasure, the chances are greater that we will notice the pleasure.

The way to train ourselves to do this is each night, make a list of specific goals and accomplishments you want to complete the next day. That sense of purpose creates energy. There is a certain adrenaline rush that comes from the anticipation of achievement. This is the same joy that exists when we are on a trip or vacation. Before we even set out we have already imagined how exciting it will be to do all the various activities we have planned. That energy should be brought into our everyday lives.

The Joy of Being Part of Something Big

There is another aspect of joy that ties us into the third category of substantive joy. Most experiences of joy have another point in common, which is the sense of feeling bigger than we were before.   Whether it is winning the lottery, getting married, finishing an important task or seeing someone we have not seen in a long time. Every instance is a realization that we are bigger than where we were before. I was poor now I am rich. I was single now I am married. I was alone now I have my friend. Connecting to something larger than ourselves is substantive joy. It is this connection that is the powerful joy that we experience from the championship game. Whether we are in the stadium with fifty thousand screaming fans or cheering from home we know that we are part of something big.

Wisdom is the Source of Joy

Ultimate joy therefore comes from identifying with something larger than myself. It comes from having a sense of meaning and a sense of purpose. It comes from an awareness that what I am doing will make a difference in this world. That is why Judaism says one of the greatest joys that can exist in this world comes from wisdom because it removes doubt from our lives. Wisdom is what gives us the ability to change the world. Without wisdom nothing can be accomplished. Building a bridge requires wisdom. Making a marriage work requires wisdom. Raising children requires wisdom. If we want to change the world, if we want to take responsibility for the world, if we want to make a difference, then we need wisdom. And once we acquire that wisdom, we should dance for joy. We should realize that we have just received the grand prize of life. We have acquired the tools to conquer our world.

This aspect of joy can be found in all areas of life. Aside from the anticipation of an opportunity and aside from tapping into something greater than where we are right now, if we seek to understand what it is that is enticing us, then we can experience the joy of wisdom. What is it that entices a person to want to win the lottery? What is it that entices a teenager to want his own car? In both cases, the answer is not the money or the car per se, but the freedom and independence that go with it. What is independence? How can I have independence? Is independence the ability to walk out the door and say goodbye without any restrictions? Is it the ability to do what I want to do, or is it the ability to do what I feel like doing? Can a slave ever have a sense of independence? Seek out that understanding. Once you have found fulfilling answers to those questions, you will have gained wisdom and you will have a greater sense of joy. This should be done with all of our experiences. At the end of the day we should look back and ask what we learned about life today. Share that wisdom with others. If every day is used to grow, then we will have a tremendous sense of achievement. Achievement and accomplishment are a source of incredible joy.

Life is filled with potential, and it is wisdom that allows us to tap into this potential. Just knowing what is possible should give each one of us a sense of joy that makes life a thrill. That joy fills us with the necessary energy and motivation to achieve important things.

Live In a State of Joy

- The natural state of existence is to be filled with joy.
- Wake up every day and say it is great to be alive!
- Don't get caught up with false joy.
- Joy comes from the pleasure of accomplishment.
- See the potential that your endeavors have to offer.
- Every day have a list of goals to accomplish.
- Wisdom is the greatest source of joy.
- At the end of every day identify one lesson you have learned about life.

SIX

Patience To Persevere: Every Effort Makes A Difference

"Nothing in the world is worth having or worth doing unless it means effort, pain, difficulty."
Theodore Roosevelt

Aside from our learned pessimism discussed earlier, another powerful obstacle stands in the way of our desire for greatness. We have an immense aversion to pain and effort. Rabbi Weinberg told me that when he was a boy his teacher would always say to him, "Noah, your challenge in life is not that you don't want to be great. You want to be great. You just want it to happen in one day and on that day you want to sleep!"

Every one of us wants to be great. The problem is that we want to just wake up great. When we see other people in positions of power and prominence we project ourselves into their place. We can easily envision being in their position and imagine how incredible that would be. Never mind that it took that person an immense amount of time, energy and resources to get there. We simply focus on the final product standing before us.

Any accomplishment takes effort. Do you remember learning how to ride a bike or drive a car? If you are like most people, the thought that you would not be able to learn this skill definitely crossed your mind at some point – especially in the early stages. Nonetheless, you pushed through and eventually managed to figure out how to stop the bike without simply falling to the side. This is true of everything. Believe it or not, some people actually know how to ride a unicycle. If we were to try, we would be convinced it was an instrument of torture. However, if we undertook to try and try again, eventually we might actually get the hang of it.

The Urge to Quit is Constant

Think about the first time you decided to exercise. It doesn't matter whether you chose to start small by jogging a mile and gradually building up your stamina or whether you dove right in and attempted five miles. The same thing would happen. Whatever distance you planned, at about the half-way point, a voice would start to ring in your head.

"What were you thinking?"

"This is absurd!"

"You need to stop!"

Determined not to quit, you pushed on. Realizing this, the voice would turn up the volume and begin to throw an increasingly absurd litany of objections, eventually bordering on the insane.

"If you don't stop running right now your left leg will fall off."

"Any moment you are going to cough and your lung will literally come pouring out."

"If you don't stop right now you will DIE!!!!"

The truth is, we are willing to convince ourselves of anything in order to be able to quit.

Pain is the Price We Pay for Pleasure

Quitting is easy. Quitting is seductive. Quitting allows us to indulge in our lust for comfort. We will do almost anything to avoid pain. If whatever we are engaged in is painful then all we have to do is just stop and the pain will go away. What we have to realize is that pain is the price we pay for pleasure. Imagine the pleasure an Olympic athlete has as the medal is being draped around his head, or what a musician feels after performing on stage and hearing the applause. If there is anything in our life that we truly appreciate, it is only because we allowed ourselves to endure a tremendous amount of pain.

Children are one of the greatest pleasures in life. At the same time, anyone with children will tell you that they are also the source of an incredible amount of pain. From the sleepless nights when they are infants to the tantrums they throw as a toddler, children continuously test our patience. Yet, those same exasperating monsters melt our hearts with pleasure. When they laugh, all the troubles of the world are forgotten. When they tell you in their soft little voice "daddy, i luv you," nothing else seems to matter. The teenager who crashes the car or gets in trouble at school (among other transgressions) is the same creature who warms your heart and says thank you for all you did for her upon graduation. Infants become toddlers, toddlers blossom into teenagers, teenagers grow to be adults and all along this train ride they are a constant source of sheer joy that comes at the cost of a tremendous amount of emotional turmoil and pain. This is true of anything worthwhile in life. The greater the pleasure, the greater the price required to receive that pleasure.

It is incredible to note that the inability to withstand this kind of pain is a learned trait. Infants and toddlers seem immune to the concept of quitting. When a three-year-old wants something, the answer no seems to have no relevance whatsoever. They will just continue to ask again and again with the keen awareness that if they just hold out long enough they will get that entire bag of chocolate in the store. If we had not been able to persist with such tenacity when we were that young, none of us would have ever learned to walk or talk. Could you imagine going through teething as an adult?

However, the physical pain we felt when we fell off our bikes pales in comparison to the pain of failing as we grow older. The thought of failing is so overwhelming that often we would rather quit before ever beginning, rather than facing the possibility of not succeeding in our efforts.

The Ability to Fall

When I was 19, I went skiing for the first time in my life. My best friend called me and invited me to go on a week-long ski trip with him and three other friends to the Larenchen Mountains in Canada. All four of them were avid skiers, while I had never even been on a mountain. I was incredibly nervous, but said yes nonetheless. We spent a week in this quaint little town nestled deep in the mountains. On our first day there, we were all standing at the bottom of the slopes. Each of them was dressed in their proper ski attire, while I was wearing jeans on top of sweat pants on top of thermals - clear signs I had no idea what I was doing. My friend told me not to worry, and that he was going to teach me everything I needed to know. At that moment, he said it was time for my first lesson. He suddenly pushed me and I fell to the ground. I was shocked to say the least. He then explained that I was going to fall a lot that day and that the first thing I needed to know was not to be afraid to fall. He was right, I did fall a lot. Several locals even thanked me for the entertainment I was providing. However, by the end of the day, after countless epic wipeouts, I was able to finally make it down the mountain without endangering everyone else on the slopes. Had I been afraid to fall I never would have learned how to ski.

The fear of failure is so strong that it can prevent a person from moving forward in life. As we discussed in the chapter on fear, many people are terrified of getting into a relationship for fear they might have their heart broken if it doesn't work out. One of the worst areas where this fear manifests itself is the inability to make decisions. We are so frightened of making the wrong choice that we end up not making any choice at all. How often do we say regarding some important decision that we need to think about it, when in truth this is just our way of avoiding the decision entirely? Instead of actually thinking about the situation, we agonize over the fact that we need to make a choice. At the last moment, by the force of a deadline, we then hastily make a choice – and hope for the best. Hardly a deliberate decision.

We have to be prepared to make mistakes in life. Mary Pickford, the cofounder of United Artists Studio and a founder of the Academy of Motion Picture Arts and Sciences, expressed it beautifully when she said, "If you have made mistakes, there is always another chance for you, for this thing we call failure, is not falling down but the staying down." There is a saying in Jewish wisdom that the righteous person falls seven times and rises. It is not simply that it is acceptable to fall, but by definition, falling is part of what makes a person great. Each unsuccessful attempt fortifies a person's resilience – as long as he gets up to battle another day.

Every Effort Makes a Difference

We previously discussed the great leader, Rabbi Akiva, in the context of his optimism. However, there is more to that story, which provides insight into this aspect of perseverance. Before Rabbi Akiva made the decision to go and become the great Rabbi Akiva, he was just Akiva the skeptic. The thought that learning Jewish wisdom would have any benefit for him seemed ludicrous at that point in his life. What changed so that he was ready to accept his future wife's offer?

One day he was taking a walk to contemplate his situation when he came across a stream of water. He sat down to think. While sitting there he noticed a spot where the water trickled over a ridge and was dripping on a rock below. The dripping water had bored a hole in the rock. Upon seeing that, Rabbi Akiva came to the conclusion that if water, which is soft, can bore a hole through a rock, which is hard, then the force and power of wisdom should certainly be able to pierce my stubborn heart, which is nothing more than flesh. At first, the obvious lesson to this story is that with patience and persistence anything is possible. However, that was not Rabbi Akiva's genius.   Rabbi Akiva's genius was that he immediately understood something that most of us refuse to accept – namely, that the expectation of instant results is foolish. Rabbi Akiva realized that even the very first drop of water must have made a difference. Otherwise, even a billion drops would have accomplished nothing. If one drop does nothing then a billion also does nothing, because a billion times zero remains zero.

Don't Look for Immediate Results

The hardest thing to accept is not merely that the results of our efforts are not what we had hoped for. Perhaps even more difficult to handle is when we make the attempt nothing seems to change at all.   The key word there is "seems." The truth is that every effort makes a difference.

Regardless of the fact that we don't always notice the fruits of our labor, every effort has an impact. My father was a pharmacist, so I grew up knowing a lot about medication. I used to have terrible allergies and back then the idea of alternative solutions was unheard of. If you sneezed you took pills. When I left for Israel to study, my father made sure I had enough allergy medication to last me some time. Since my one year trip turned into a seven year journey I eventually ran out. I took the empty bottle to a local Jerusalem pharmacy to see if there was some Israeli equivalent for the medication that I could get without a prescription. I don't know if what the pharmacist told me is true or not, but the point is quite insightful. She provided me with something to take, and warned me that I would not notice the results right away. I asked her why she was telling me that. She said that Americans need instant results, and therefore the American medications are made to have a strong initial impact, but do not last as long; this medicine, on the other hand, will not be noticed as quickly, but will have much more lasting results.

Again, I don't know if what she said was pharmaceutically true, but the lesson hit home. We are so focused on instant results and instant success that we get frustrated and want to quit when they don't happen immediately. We must remember that everything takes time. But not only do things take time, every effort we make, in and of itself, makes a difference. We need to remember this especially when we do not notice it. Thomas Edison said, "Many of life's failures are simply people who did not realize how close they were to success when they gave up." It is crucial to look back every now and then to see how far we have come and take pleasure in our accomplishments. Appreciate that those accomplishments took time, and that every effort made a difference. If we refuse to quit and continue to put in the effort then that alone is changing our world.

Every Effort Counts

- The urge to quit is constant.
- You're not going to die by trying, but quitting will kill your soul.
- Make a list of achievements you appreciate in life and realize how much effort and pain you went through to get them.
- Don't be afraid to fail.
- Our failures are simply the steps that take us to the next success.
- No matter what the outcome is, it made a difference.
- There is no instant gratification when it comes to success.

SEVEN

Unity: Humility Is The Key To The Greatest Power

> *"Pride is concerned with who is right. Humility is concerned with what is right."*
> **Ezra Taft Benson**

There is a force that exists that allows us to achieve what others see as impossible. It is the final ingredient necessary to help us to break through all the barriers that confine us to the perceived limitations of this world. That force is called unity. Helen Keller said, "Alone we can do so little and together we can do so much!" If people would just work together, obstacles that seem insurmountable tend to dissipate.

Unity is the single most powerful force in the universe. Unity is not just having more people doing the same thing. Two people together can lift more than just double the weight. It is written in the Torah that when we have unity, five will be able to chase away a hundred enemies, while a hundred will chase ten thousand. Unity is exponential! That is the power of unity and it is unstoppable.

In the Biblical story of the Tower of Babel, humanity united to build a tower. The complex reasons for the tower and the people's understanding of what it would accomplish are beyond the scope of this book. Suffice it to say that the main premise was a glorification of man's accomplishments and the elimination of any need for God. Now imagine you are God. You have all the powers of the Almighty at your disposal, and humanity attempts to make you irrelevant by means of this tower. How would you respond? It seems to me that the most obvious thing to do would simply be to destroy the tower. And if that seems to be too lenient of a response for such insolent behavior, then push the reset button, wipe them out, and start over. Keep in mind that this is exactly what was done in the story of Noah and the flood which took place immediately prior in the Torah's narrative.

However, this time God responds in an entirely different manner. Since mankind used unity for the wrong purpose, God removed unity from mankind. The power of unity had become so set in the consciousness of humanity that the idea of the Tower was bound to resurface – and with it the same intent of making God irrelevant. Therefore, God created different languages, which left groups of people unable to communicate with each other. Construction of the Tower came to a halt. As a result, it would now be possible for new ideas to come into the world. These new ideas would help broaden humanity's understanding of life. Eventually, the original intention of humanity's ultimate unity would return, but only through the creation of temporary discord. Otherwise, the single-minded outlook they had would have become a permanent and destructive fixture of human thought.

Humility Leads to Unity

The way to achieve this type of unity is through humility. Unity comes about through a recognition that the whole is greater than the sum of its parts. Thomas Edison was asked why he had a team of 21 assistants. He said, "If I could solve all the problems myself, I would." Unity comes when we appreciate that the power of the group is greater than I am. I have to be willing to accept that I don't know everything. I have to be open to hearing other people's ideas. If I always think I am right, then it is always about me. It is not about creating unity. If we truly want to achieve greatness then we must see past ourselves and focus on the big picture.

The 2004 movie *Miracle* depicts the story of the 1980 US Olympic hockey team. To put things in historical perspective, America and Russia were in the thick of the Cold War. The Russian hockey team was an undefeated powerhouse. The thought that the United States could beat the Russians that year was far from reality. Instead, most people were hoping the team would survive without being humiliated. The coach, Herb Brooks, saw it very differently. He wanted to win. He knew that the United States would only be able to beat the Russians if they played as a unified team.

There is an incredibly intense scene in the movie in which the US team plays an exhibition game against Norway. Even though they win, the coach forces them to skate exercise drills right after the game. To set up the dramatic climax of this scene, throughout the film Coach Brooks had asked players to state their name and who they play for. Each time a different player would say his name and the college he played for. During the drills after the Norway game, the players were exhausted and seemed to be at the limit of their physical capabilities. Coach Brooks lectures them that if they think they can beat the Russians on their talent alone, then they are hugely mistaken. "You don't have enough talent," he declares. This barrage of rebuke continues until finally, breathless and weak, Mike Eruzione calls out his name. Coach Brooks then asks him who he plays for.

"I play for the United States of America," Mike proclaims.

At that moment Coach Brooks says that they are free to go. This actually happened in real life. The dialogue and climax of the scene are a creation of Hollywood; in real life they stopped when Coach Brooks thought they had had enough. Even though this dialogue was a creation of Hollywood the point rings true. Until that point the players were focused on themselves – look at me, I made it to the Olympics. Therefore, they said they played for their own college. It was only when they realized they were not playing for themselves, but for something much bigger, that they were ready to beat the Russians. They were playing for the United States of America. The reason the film is called *Miracle* is because the United States team went on to beat the Russians, and win the gold. In the final seconds of the game, the famous sports announcer Al Michaels said, "Do you believe in miracles?" When there is unity present miracles can happen.

Unity of Purpose Versus Unity of Being

Unity exists in two forms. One type of unity is the result of a shared goal. The classic example of this is a sports team. If a team lacks unity, it is unlikely that they will be successful. This kind of unity is dependent on the goal. Once the goal is completed, however, the unity ceases to exist.

The second type of unity is much more profound. That is unity of being. Unity of being comes as a result of sharing our souls with others. It means allowing ourselves to be vulnerable and exposing our thoughts, dreams and emotions. The difference between these two types of unity is that the latter allows a couple to go from merely living together and performing the functions of a working home to becoming one.

One of the key building blocks of any relationship is intimacy. Intimacy is defined as the ability to expose ourselves in a way that brings closeness. Some people have no problem exposing themselves, but that doesn't necessarily endear them to anyone else. These are people who often reveal too much about themselves too early in a relationship. Others are extremely uneasy when it comes to opening up and allowing someone else inside. They create a wall that keeps everyone at bay. Both of these are detrimental to building solid intimacy in a relationship. Instead, we must be prepared to open ourselves up to others. We must be willing to expose ourselves to a level of vulnerability that will allow others in. Unity of being can only be achieved by intimacy.

This second and much deeper level of unity is rare because we get caught up in caring about how we are perceived by others. So much energy is wasted worrying about what someone said about me or how I was treated. Our egos are so fragile that the slightest infraction against us can ruin not just one day, but several days, if not months, and sometimes, tragically, years. How many families are torn apart, with siblings not speaking to each other because of something one of them may or may not have said or even meant. When we care so much about what others think of us, then it is only natural that our focus is not on making sure we do the right thing. Rather, we are preoccupied on doing things that will make us loved by others.

The Need to Be Loved and Have Self Respect

The challenge here is that being loved is a basic human need. So much of who we are and our confidence in life is built on the extent to which we know we are loved. If we go back to the chapter on optimism, we will find the key to this awareness. One of the basic elements of optimism was built around the understanding that everything that happens is for the best because God loves us. Knowing that God loves me should allow me to have another love which is more crucial than anyone else's love or recognition – the ability to love myself.

According to Judaism, having a sense of self-worth and love of oneself is an obligation. Probably the most widely recognized and valued commandment is to Love

Your Neighbor as Yourself. Explicit in that commandment is the understanding that we must love ourselves before we are truly able to love others.

The only way to stop caring about what others think of me is to know that I am worthy of being loved. One of the greatest obstacles to greatness is that we don't view ourselves of being worthy of achieving such heights.   So many great leaders throughout history viewed themselves as unworthy of the task. Even Moses argued at length with God that he was not the right choice for the job. Once those individuals realized that what they thought about themselves was irrelevant they were able to move forward.

Having unity of being can only come once we have unity within ourselves. We must be able to recognize who we are and appreciate our talents as well as our faults. This does not mean being comfortable with our shortcomings and resigning ourselves to mediocrity. Instead, it means recognizing that we don't have to live up to some glorified image of who we think we ought to be right now. We can and should have an aspiration of becoming greater than we are, but also be at peace and love ourselves for where we have come to so far. At the same time, loving oneself is not a license for arrogance. We must learn to see ourselves as having value while maintaining our sense of humility.

Humility is Power

Seeing ourselves as unworthy is actually the antithesis of humility. People often misunderstand humility. A humble person is not someone who thinks negatively of himself. On the contrary, true humility gives a person a tremendous sense of power. Moses was the most humble man ever to live. Here is a man that had the courage to challenge the most powerful dictator alive, Pharaoh. Pharaoh viewed himself as a god. Moses marched right up to him and declared, "Let my people go!" Imagine standing up to Kim Jong-Un in the capital of North Korea without any military escort and demanding that he cease his terrorist activities. That is precisely what Moses did. Moses went right into the palace with no more than a walking stick and his brother by his side. This is not the image of a timid man. The sheer confidence that Moses must have had is mind blowing. Yet, his ability to do this was quite simple. Moses understood that this had nothing to do with him. This was going to happen because God told him so. Moses was humble, because he had the clarity to know that he and his self-image were not the determining factor of what he should or should not do in life. Moses understood that the only thing that mattered was doing the right thing.

When we have the ability to be objective, it is only natural that we will have humility. Once we remove our personal agendas or desires, we can then ask ourselves what is the right thing to do. It does not matter how I will be viewed as a result or how my stature will be affected. The only thing that matters is getting the job done. When our focus is directed this way we can have unity as well. It will not be relevant whose idea it is or who is able to do what. If someone has a better idea, I want to hear it. If someone has more talent, then let him do the task. Phil Jackson, the famous basketball coach of both the Chicago Bulls and Los Angeles Lakers, said that if a coach wants to win he must be willing to accept eighty percent of his vision one hundred percent of the time. Everyone sees his ideas as the best. Everyone naturally thinks he can do it better than anyone else. However, it is not possible for one person to play every position and to do every task. Therefore, in order to succeed we must be willing to accept that maybe we don't have the best vision. Maybe someone can do it better. And if I need to let go of some of my personal agendas to achieve that, then so be it.

Humility is the key to achieving unity and actualizing that power. A person with true humility understands that if the focus and effort are directed purely at achieving the ultimate good, then that goal is inevitable. This is that deeper utilization of free will mentioned in a previous chapter. Before our goal was to get past the body's desire for comfort and identify with the soul's quest for meaning and accomplishment. The next level is to connect with the idea that we are not merely a soul. Rather, we are a spark of the Infinite. If the Almighty is behind our efforts then we can't be stopped. As Ronald Reagan said, "I truly believe that good always triumphs in the end." That level of clarity and humility is power.

Humility and Unity

- One person can change the world. He just can't do it alone.
- It's not about me. It's about what needs to get done.
- Get rid of your ego because it only prevents you from allowing others into your life who can help you succeed.
- Don't do things to be loved and accepted, rather, do things because they are right and love yourself because you know you have value and self-respect.
- True humility is an understanding that when we do good we have power that far surpasses all other forces in the universe.

We Can Change The World

"Here's to the crazy ones...because the ones who are crazy enough to think that they can change the world, are the ones who do."
Steve Jobs

These seven traits are by no means a complete list of positive attributes a person should strive to attain. Every human being should be kind, giving, compassionate, etc. Every one of us should constantly endeavor to become better individuals by working on all of our character traits. Life needs to be a constant state of minimizing our negative habits and faulty character traits, while at the same time building and nurturing our positive virtues. The journey to becoming great has many tracks. This book focused primarily on the quest of taking responsibility for the world on both the micro and macro levels because the tools necessary are the same for both.

This world was created in a state of perfect imperfection. The deficiencies of the world are there precisely to make us great as we go about rectifying them. The ultimate utopian image we all have of the world comes from the description of the Garden of Eden, the original state of paradise in which mankind lived. What we often forget is that the snake was part of that creation. The existence of that which needed to be changed was also present in paradise. The goal of changing the world, striving for a state of perfection is intrinsic to the very quest of life itself. It is that journey that brings us fulfillment.

If we want to change our world there is one additional aspect that is a prerequisite to these seven traits. We have to care. If we care then we will find a way but if we don't care then nothing will motivate or change us. Find something that you truly care about and then dedicate your life to making an impact in that. These seven traits will then provide the tools necessary to accomplish. Begin by seeking total clarity. We must have five-finger clarity on what our life's priorities are, and why we are embarking on that mission. We have to be just as clear on what we hope to achieve. We must realize that we alone are responsible for our lives, and embrace that obligation. Abdicating this responsibility brings serious consequences in its wake. Likewise, choosing to change the world brings great reward. Regardless of what the outcome is, it is always for our best, but we must also have the confidence that we can be successful. We can change our world for the better, because if the Almighty helps us, then there is nothing we cannot accomplish. Life is beautiful, and when we realize that, the weight of life will be lifted. Focus both on past milestones, as well as the potential of the future. This will give you the necessary energy to push on. Greatness does not come overnight. However, with every effort we make, our lives are profoundly impacted, even though we may not realize this at first. Finally, if we work on our humility, we will have unity within ourselves and with others, and together we can change the world.

Notes

INTRODUCTION. LEARNING TO FLY

The idea of ten being the number significant enough to make such a dramatic change comes from the Biblical story of Sodom and Gemorah (see Genesis Chapter 18, verses 17-33). When Abraham was told that the cities were to be destroyed he debated with God to save those cities. Abraham began by asking if there were 50 righteous people. He chose 50 because in addition to those two cities there were three other smaller cities. Abraham argued that as long as there were ten righteous people in each city they could change the wicked ways of the rest of the populace. He reduced the number by five assuming he could play a role as one of the ten for each city. When that didn't work he eliminated one city at a time reducing the number by ten. In the end none of the cities had ten righteous men.

The Babylonian Talmud states in *Sanhedrin* folio 37a that a person is obligated to say "the world was created for me". This is based on the world having been created for a single human in the story of creation. In that context we are to understand that if someone takes a human life it is as if they have destroyed an entire world. Conversely, saving a life is equivalent to saving an entire world.

ONE. FIVE FINGER CLARITY

In Genesis Chapter 2, verse 8, Adam is placed in the garden immediately after he was created and given a soul. Subsequently, in Chapter 2, verse 15, it states explicitly that God takes Adam and places him in the garden. Seemingly Adam is taken out of the garden only to be put back in the very same place! The instructions "to work it and to guard it" are given in verse 15. The hebrew word for place in verse 8 is וישם, whereas the word used in verse 15 is וינחהו. The latter comes from the root to rest. Life in the garden was the epitome of paradise, the work that Adam was being instructed to do was not laborious farming. Similarly, there were no external threats to the garden that he needed to worry about and protect the garden from. The real work necessary in the garden was to exert effort in learning from the garden, seek out wisdom from the world around him and learn about life. It should be obvious, therefore, that the threat Adam had to guard the garden from was himself and his own corruption.

Rabbi Moshe Chaim Luzzatto wrote the Path of the Just in 1740 in Amsterdam. It is probably his most influential work, studied in virtually every Rabbinical Institute. The aim of the work is the perfection of character. The entire work is based on a single statement of a Sage from the Talmudic era; Rabbi Pinchas Ben-Yair; "Torah leads to watchfulness; watchfulness leads to alacrity; alacrity leads to cleanliness; cleanliness leads to abstention; abstention leads to purity; purity leads to piety; piety leads to humility; humility leads to fear of sin; fear of sin leads to holiness; holiness leads to prophecy; prophecy leads to resurrection of the dead". (Babylonian Talmud *Avodah Zarah* folio 20b) Each of these steps takes up several chapters with explanation, various elements, how to acquire them and what detracts one from achieving them.

The story of Abraham and Nimrod is found in the Rabbinical literature (see *Midrash Rabbah* Chapter 38 Paragraph 13). At first Nimrod commands Abraham to worship fire. Abraham responds that it would be better to worship water which is clearly more powerful than fire. Nimrod tells him to worship the water. Abraham then claims that it would be better to bow down to clouds which are stronger since they have the ability to carry water. Nimrod agrees. Abraham then explains that wind is much stronger than clouds from the fact that wind can scatter and dissipate clouds. Nimrod demands that he worship the wind. Abraham then asks if he should simply worship a person since humans can stand up and withstand the wind. At that point Nimrod realizes that Abraham is merely mocking him and demands that he either worship the fire or be thrown in. Interestingly, Abraham's brother, Haran, was also there. His brother said to himself if Abraham survives I will say I am with him and if he does not I will say I am with Nimrod. After Abraham survived, Haran was asked if he also follows Abraham's views. He confidently declared yes. They took him and threw him into the furnace and he died.

The image of the mountain versus the anthill is described in the Babylonian Talmud *Succah* folio 52a. There it discusses the *Yetzer Hara*, the voice inside each one of us that tries to prevent us from achieving greatness. That voice will ultimately be destroyed and laid out in front of us to see. In the same place, it is said the the Almighty is also shocked at those of us who failed to conquer it since He gave us the tools and capabilities to do so. One of the Sages warns us that the image of the thread of hair is how the voice always begins. If we have the fortitude to conquer it at that time it will be much easier. Later, it will only get stronger and stronger.

TWO. RESPONSIBILITY

The story of Elijah and the fisherman appears in the Rabbinical literature *Tanna D'vei Eliyahu*. Ultimately all of the excuses are directed at the Almighty. This is precisely the same defense that Adam used when confronted by God as to why he ate from the tree. "The woman you gave me, she gave me the fruit and I ate" (Genesis Chapter 3, verse 12). On the surface he seems to be blaming Eve but in truth what Adam is really saying is that his sin was God's fault. God was the one who put the woman here causing me to be deceived.

In Deuteronomy Chapter 30, verses 15 - 19, the Torah delineates that the choice is between life and death. The verses begin with the statement that life and good on one hand, death and evil on the other, have been placed before us. Then again in verse 19 it states that life and death, blessing and curse have been placed before us. The choices therefore are between life, good and blessing on one side with death, evil and curse on the other. The Torah summarizes this choice by simply stating "choose life". The choice between good and evil or blessing and curse is not a choice. We always choose good over evil and blessing over curse. Even when what we choose is clearly not good nor a blessing we convince ourselves that it is. Death however is a choice that is always present. Even when we choose momentary death we rationalize that it is for our good.

Genesis Chapter 18, verses 1 through 8, open up with God appearing before Abraham at the entrance to his tent. The very next verse says that Abraham looked out beyond the tent and saw three men approaching. He then begged them to come in so he could offer them some food. This incident took place immediately after Abraham's circumcision. God was coming to Abraham to visit him and offer some comfort. This is one of the instances where the Babylonian Talmud *Sotah* folio 14a states that we should emulate

God; just as He visits the sick so should we. Now in order to allow Abraham the ability to rest and heal, the day had been made extremely hot. This way there would be no one traveling that Abraham would want to cater to. When it became clear that Abraham was caused more anguish by his inability to host guests, God saw that sending guests would be an even greater comfort to Abraham. Taking care of guests, which is ultimately taking care of humanity, is praised on many levels. (See the Babylonian Talmud *Shabbat* folio 127a.)

THREE. FEAR:
LIVE WITH THE REALITY OF CONSEQUENCES

Both the hebrew word for fear and the hebrew word to see share the same spelling; יראה. Additionally in Proverbs Chapter 1, verse 7, and Chapter 9, verse 10, it states that fear is the beginning of knowledge and wisdom. To see consequences to our actions is a sign of maturity and understanding about life.

In *Ethics of the Fathers* Chapter 2, Paragraph 10, the Sage Rabbi Eliezer says that we should correct our ways the day before we die. His students asked (Babylonian Talmud *Shabbat* folio 153a) how does one know what day they are going to die that they should correct their ways on the day before?! He responded that is precisely the point. Since we don't know the day of our death, we should correct our ways every day, since tomorrow might very well be that day. (Also Proverbs Chapter 27 verse 1, we don't know what tomorrow will be)

FOUR. OPTIMISM: EVERYTHING THAT HAPPENS
IS FOR THE BEST

In regards to Rabbi Akiva's leadership it is worth noting that many of the greatest early Sages of the Talmud were Rabbi Akiva's students. The incident where the Sages came upon the Temple's destruction is found in the Babylonian Talmud *Makkos* folios 24a - 24b. The prophecies he referred to are Micah Chapter 3, verse 12 and Zechariah Chapter 8, verse 4. (See Babylonian Talmud *Berachos* folio 60b - 60a for when he was locked out of the city, Babylonian Talmud *Pesachim* folio 49b for his views prior to learning, Babylonian Talmud *Kesuvos* folios 62b - 63a for the marriage to Rachel, the daughter of Ben Savua.)

The seven steps are based on Rabbi Weinberg's approach to the philosophical work Duties of the Heart, 4th Gate by Rabbi Bachya Evan Pakuah written around the year 1040 in Spain.

FIVE. JOY: SEE THE POTENTIAL

The story of Cain and Abel is in Genesis Chapter 4, verses 1 thorough 16. There are numerous lessons that can be learned from this story but an additional one that relates to joy is the fact that Cain killed Abel. Instead of Cain improving himself his response to Abel being better was very simple; kill him. When someone cares about being number one there will always be someone else that prevents them from being happy and joyful. There will always be someone better. Instead of focussing on becoming better, to often the response is "kill" the competition. Negate their achievements or destroy their character in our mind and we've killed the competition thereby becoming number one in our own mind by default.

See *Metzudas Dovid* on Proverbs Chapter 15, verse 30, for joy coming as a result of the removal of doubt.

SIX. PATIENCE TO PERSEVERE: EVERY EFFORT MAKES A DIFFERENCE

The sage Rabbi Shimon Ben Levi said in the Babylonian Talmud *Kiddushin* folio 30b that the *Yetzer Hara* (as defined in a previous note) gets stronger each day and seeks to kill us.

The sage Ben Hei Hei said in *Ethics of the Fathers* Chapter 5, Paragraph 21 that according to the pain is the reward. Pain is to be understood as the effort.

Rabbi Akiva pondering over the water dripping on the rock can be found in the Rabbinical literature *Avos D'Rabbi Nosson.*

SEVEN. UNITY: HUMILITY IS THE KEY TO THE GREATEST POWER

The verse showing the exponential power of unity is in Leviticus Chapter 26, verse 8.

The story of the Tower of Babel is in Genesis Chapter 11, verses 1 through 9. The unity that existed in the story of Tower of Babel occurred two more times in the Torah, albeit with individual nations not the entire world. There are only two instances where an entire nation is referred to using a singular verb form as opposed to plural. The first is when the Egyptians chased the Jewish people to the sea, only to ultimately perish. The second is when the Jewish people were unified at Mount Sinai. One unity led to a nation's demise whereas the other was the enabler to bring wisdom into the world. In both instances the force of unity was immense and able to change an entire nation's history and the entire world's destiny. (see Exodus Chapter 14, verse 10, and Chapter 19, verse 2).

Acknowledgments

When Rabbi Weinberg became ill I decided I was going to focus all my teaching on the wisdom I had learned from him. One day during that time I was asked to teach a class for another Rabbi. This class was comprised of incredibly intelligent and successful businessmen. I decided to teach them the seven traits. For some time I had merely incorporated the ideas into all my various classes but never as a topic on their own. At the conclusion of the class they all remarked at how powerful the ideas were and that I should continue presenting them on their own. If I need to begin my thanks somewhere then I should probably thank Rabbi Nachum Braverman for inviting me to teach that day and "The Minyan" group for their assurance that this material was indeed powerful. In particular from that group, thank you Tommy and Eddie for welcoming me into your office and giving me a space to call my own. I am humbled every time I sit in your father's office. I cherish our friendship.

My next thanks must go to all my students. While I was fortunate and blessed enough to have a relationship with Rabbi Weinberg it is only through teaching that any of his wisdom became real. The Sages have a saying; "from my teachers I learned a lot, from my colleagues I learned even more but from my students I learned the most." Specifically I want to thank my Whiskey and Wisdom group for their years of loyalty and love. You guys are very dear to me and my family. A few select students were kind enough to read through the many drafts of this book and offer invaluable edits, suggestions and feedback. Special thanks among them go to Soheil and Jonathan.

I am incredibly grateful to the brothers of Alpha Epsilon Pi Fraternity, Andrew Borans the Executive Director and Past International President Elan Carr. For the past fourteen years I have had the opportunity to cultivate and test these ideas on thousands of the finest and brightest young men. Proud to be a Pi.

Thank you Richard Horowitz and family. Your continued immeasurable support throughout the years is only matched by your enduring trust and confidence in all of my efforts and accomplishments.

The thought of putting these ideas into a book started many years ago. Because I succumbed to much of the naysaying spoken about in this book I never thought I would be able to do it. After attempting on numerous occasions to have others write it for me I finally listened to the wisdom of the 7 Traits and began writing it myself. I have to thank Saul Blinkoff, my passionate student and dear friend for constantly reminding me to just get this done. Thank you to Rabbi David Ordan for editing this and making it grammatically coherent. Thank you Jay Klein and your incredible team at Pur-Gum for your marketing insights and design help with the cover.

It should seem obvious that I am forever indebted to Rabbi Weinberg for sharing his wisdom with me. He was such a unique individual that there is no way for me to summarize or express my thanks to him. I must say this though, it is a special gift to have someone in your life who believes in you and has the wisdom and understanding to teach you how to believe in yourself as well.

I never would have met Rabbi Weinberg if it wasn't for my dearest friend in the world, Aryeh Kornbleuth. I owe him more than can ever be written in several book acknowledgments.

Whenever I think of a man, I think of my father. I was so blessed to have had him as a father. I miss him so much and would have loved for him to have seen me complete something.

I could not begin to imagine being a man if it wasn't for my wife, Nechama. As the Sages say "any man without a wife is not a man". Thank you for making me a man.

Finally, I have to thank the Almighty for giving me the gift of life and the opportunity to take responsibility for my world.

Epilogue: A Woman Wants A Man

Throughout this book, we have focused on acquiring the seven traits as they apply to changing the world irrespective of gender. However, there is something unique and intrinsic about these traits and taking responsibility for one's world that is the embodiment of what it means to be specifically a man. A man's essence encompasses more than simply acting on the world stage. To fully realize his human potential, a man must also take on the responsibility of building a family along with his wife. When a woman looks for such a man, she instinctively searches for someone who possesses these seven traits. Personality and chemistry are certainly important, but those alone will not build a relationship. Clarity and conviction give a man confidence, which is always high on the list of what women look for in a man. When a man lives with a sense of responsibility, a woman knows she can rely on him to take care of her and their family. Loyalty and love mandate a desire not to cause pain to someone we care about. Avoiding that harm can only come from an awareness of consequences. The optimistic man will always see the woman in his life as the perfect partner in the enterprise of building a life. A man who was unhappy before being in a relationship will remain unhappy, even when he is in a relationship. A man filled with joy will never blame his wife for his misery, because his outlook on life comes from within himself. Relationships take an enormous amount of work, and the urge to quit and run is all too present. A man with patience to persevere will never abandon his most cherished relationship. He will always be willing to work on it again and again. Ultimately, a woman desires nothing more than to have intimacy and unity with the man in her life, and that can only happen if he is humble, willing to be vulnerable and striving to create the same unity with her. That is what it means to be a man.

Made in the USA
Monee, IL
03 December 2019

17864679R00074